COMBAT COLOURS No.1
The Messerschmitt
on the Western Front

Written and illustrated by Peter Scott

The objective of this book is to document the colour schemes carried by the *Luftwaffe*'s Messerschmitt Bf 109E fleet on the 'Western Front' throughout 1940. This period encompassed the 'Phoney War' ('Sitzkrieg'); the assaults on Denmark and Norway; the offensive on France and the Low Countries; and the Battle of Britain.

Many other works have covered *Luftwaffe* colour schemes in detail, so by way of an introduction, I would like to explain how the colour schemes of the following profiles were established. This preamble therefore takes a slightly different perspective from previous works.

The aircraft
During the time period under review, the E sub-type of the Messerschmitt 109 was the current derivative of a single-engined fighter design that had first flown in 1935. The various sub-types were denoted by an alphabetic suffix, which related to progressive power plant and armament improvements. The type was already combat-proven, forty-five or so examples having been deployed in its C and D variants as part of Germany's *'Condor Legion'*, during the Spanish Civil War.

Although generally referred to as the Me 109, particularly within the Royal Air Force, the aircraft is more correctly

Heading: Werner Machold's 'yellow 5' of 9./JG 2, almost certainly at Cherbourg-Querqueville, circa August 1940. Note the twenty-three *abschussbalken* (kills) on the rudder and overpainted white areas on the fuselage cross. (M W Payne Collection)

Right: Summer 1940 - Stab III/JG 51 being refuelled in a field. The nearest aircraft is that of the Technical Officer. Note that there appears to be no bar behind the fuselage cross to signify III Gruppe, only the badge below the cockpit. (M W Payne)

defined as Bf 109. This is an abbreviation of Bayerische Flugzeugwerk AG, its original manufacturers. The company was renamed as Messerschmitt AG in 1938. Examination of wrecked aircraft during the course of the research for this book, confirmed the Bf 109 format, since the aircraft type was always stamped onto the manufacturers' plate.

During the period under consideration, the earlier variants, Bf 109Bs and Ds, had generally been relegated to training and second-line duties and the predominant front-line service type was the Bf 109E.

During 1940, the *Luftwaffe* operated the E-1, E-3 and E-4 sub-types, with deliveries of the E-7 entering service by the end of the year. Early deliveries of pre-production Bf 109F-0 sub-types were also made in late 1940 and although these were flown under combat conditions over southern England in the autumn, they fall outside the specific scope of this book.

Sub-type differences
From the point of view of interpreting photographs from the period, the distinctive physical features of the various operational sub-types were:-

- E-1 - two 7.92mm calibre MG 17 machine guns mounted in the upper engine cowling, with two more in the wings. It would appear that many E-1s were up-gunned, either at unit level or back at the factory and/or maintenance units, when undergoing major servicing work, with MG FF 20mm cannon in the wings.
- E-3 - two MG 17 machine guns mounted in the upper engine cowling, with two MG FF 20mm cannon in the wings. There was a bulged fairing on the under surfaces of each wing, to accommodate the drum magazine and ammunition feed mechanism.

Technically, there was also provision for one MG FF/M cannon firing through the engine block, but it is very doubtful if any operational aircraft were fitted with this weapon.

- E-4 - two MG 17 machine guns mounted in the upper engine cowling, with two MG FF/M 20mm cannon in the wings, with the associated wing bulges. The provision for the unreliable engine mounted MG FF/M cannon was deleted.

The E-4 was the first sub-type to be fitted with the heavily-framed flat-sided 'square' canopy and associated

windscreen. This improvement was frequently retro-fitted to earlier aircraft, so it does not provide a consistent recognition feature, as will be seen from examination of some of the later profiles.

During the course of the Battle of Britain, armour plating was attached to the canopies of all sub-types, in order to provide head protection for the pilot.

The aircraft were also capable of being fitted with a bomb rack under the fuselage. These racks were either the ETC 500 - capable of carrying one SC 250 or SD 250 (250kg) bomb, or the ETC 50 - capable of carrying four SC 50 (50kg) bombs. During the course of the Battle of Britain, *Reichmarschall* Hermann Goering ordered that one *Staffel* from each *Gruppe* should have fighter-bomber (*Jagdbomber* or *Jabo*) capability and, when these racks were fitted, the aircraft gained an additional suffix, ie '/B', eg Bf 109E-1/B.

The aircraft gained another suffix if powered by the DB 601N engine, rather than the normal DB 601A - eg Bf 109E-4/N. Although several aircraft have been illustrated as /N variants in the profile section, the improved engine remains unidentifiable from an external examination of the aircraft.

Luftwaffe unit structure

At this stage, it might be appropriate to consider the structure of the *Luftwaffe* single-engine fighter force, *Jagdverbande*, at operational level, because the colour schemes that were carried hinge upon this area.

The basic *Luftwaffe* tactical operational unit was the *Geschwader* - broadly equivalent to an RAF Group. The Fighter *Geschwader*, ie *Jagdgeschwader*, abbreviated to JG, consisted of three *Gruppen* (Wings), which in turn was made up of three *Staffeln* (Squadrons). Some *Geschwadern*, especially towards the end of the Battle of Britain, added a fourth *Staffel* to some of its *Gruppen*, which caused some re-adjustments in the *Staffel* numbering procedure, (as might be deduced from the accompanying table).

Each *Gruppe* had a *Stabsschwarm* (Staff Flight), ostensibly of four aircraft which included the *Gruppen Kommandeur*, and usually the unit Adjutant and Technical Officer, who were generally pilots. However, not all members of the *Gruppe* staff were necessarily pilots, and often non-staff rank pilots, including experienced NCOs flew with the *Stabsschwarm*.

The *Geschwader* also had a *Stabsschwarm* - the *Geschwaderstab* - led by the *Geschwader Kommodore*, and again consisting of four aircraft and generally including the *Geschwader* Adjutant and *Geschwader* Technical Officer, plus experienced pilots, again that could be drawn from any of the *Staffeln* within the *Geschwader*.

With some twelve to sixteen aircraft in a fully up-to-strength *Staffel*, the total strength of an average *Jagdgeschwader* could have anything been between 100 to 150 or so aircraft, incuding the *Stabsschwarme* - on paper. Actual operational strength varied considerably, and the average serviceable figure would have been somewhat lower.

The 'in-flight' formations were invariably based on the *Schwarm*, spaced out in the now classic 'finger four' formation - (ie reproducing the effect of the four finger tips of an outstretched hand) - of two *Rotte* (ie leader and wingman - see Fig 1). A *Staffel* flying between eight to sixteen aircraft - depending on serviceability - (in two, three, or four *Schwarme*), would formate with other *Staffeln* within the *Gruppe*, usually accompanied by the *Gruppe Stabsschwarm*, and if within the same geographical area, the *Geschwaderstab*. It was comparatively rare for a full *Jagdgeschwader* to fly together 'en masse' as individual *Gruppen* were often based miles apart on different airfields and perhaps had different operational orders - such as close escort, acting as top cover, or even on occasions in the '*Frei Jagd*' (free hunting) role.

Each *Staffel* was numbered independently within its *Gruppe*, as were the *Gruppen* within their *Geschwader*. When written down for administative purposes however, the *Gruppe* number, (identified by roman numerals), wasn't normally mentioned, because the *Staffel* number, (identified by arabic numerals), indicated to which *Gruppe* the *Staffel* belonged. (see Fig 1)

For example:- 9./JG 3 = 9 *Staffel*, of

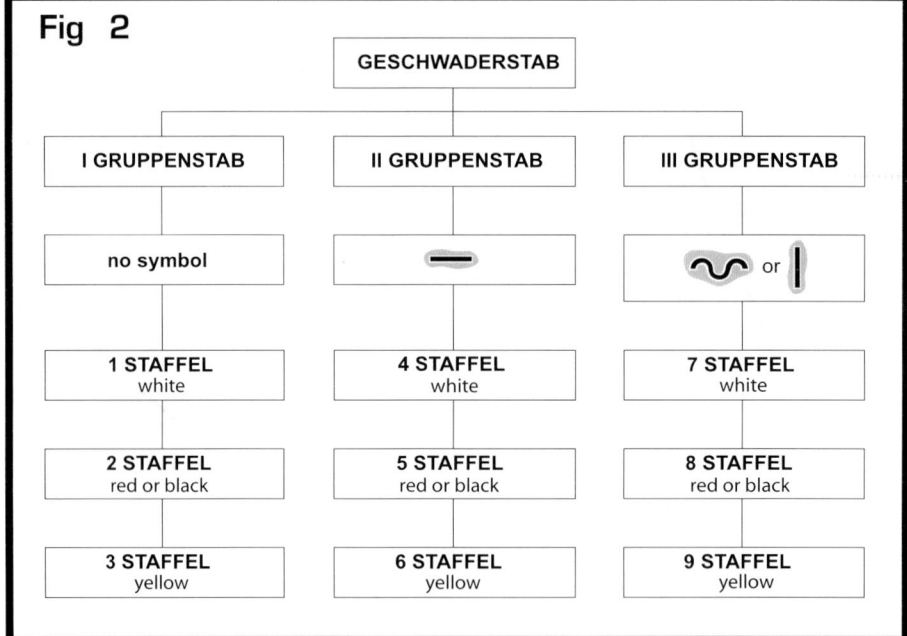

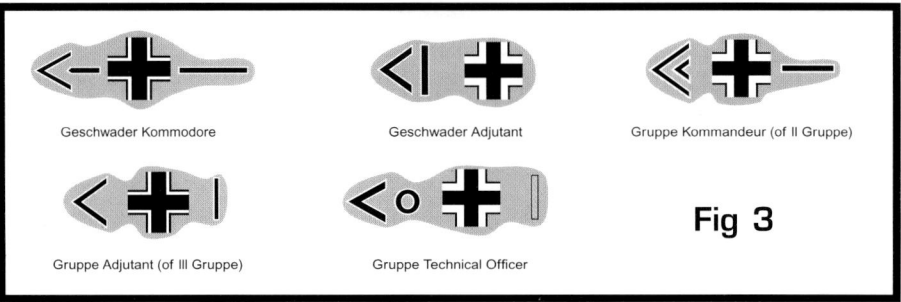

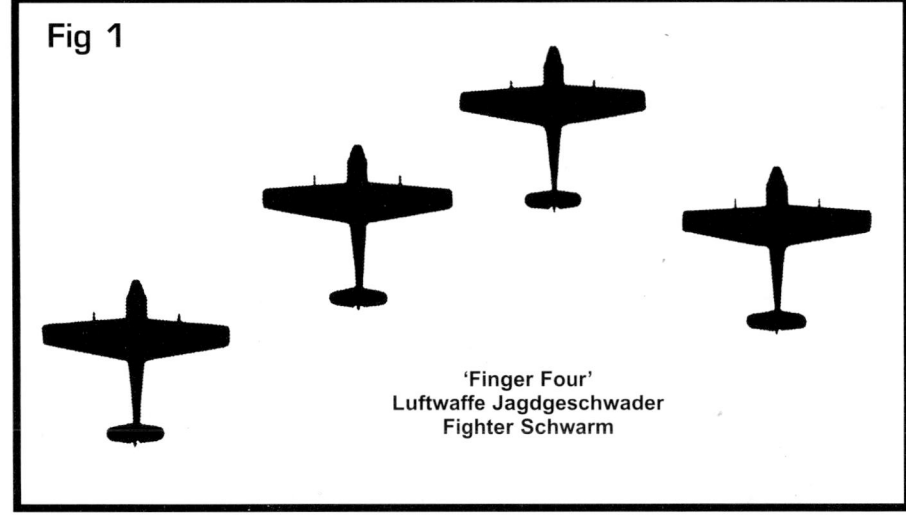

'Finger Four' Luftwaffe Jagdgeschwader Fighter Schwarm

Left and below: Two photographs of Karl Raisinger's Bf 109E-4 of 2./JG 77, which crashed at Harvey's Cross, Telscombe, Sussex on 25 October 1940. The machine was put on display in Maidstone in aid of the local "Spitfire Fund'. This aircraft may have been 'brown 13', but it is more likely to have been 'red 13'.
(M W Payne Collection left, and Kent Messenger below)

III *Gruppe*, of *Jagdgeschwader* 3.

Individual aircraft within a *Staffel* were marked with a numeral, (or in some cases a letter), in the *Staffel* colour, often but not always, outlined in a contrasting colour. These numerals were generally placed immediately in front of the fuselage cross (both sides), but occasionally were carried on the engine cowling, eg 7 and 9./JG 27, or under the widscreen, eg 7 and 8./JG 54.

The *Staffel* colours were white for the first *Staffeln* of each *Gruppe* - 1, 4 and 7;

initially red for the second *Staffeln* - 2, 5 and 8 - but in mid-1940, an anomaly not only peculiar to the Battle of Britain period but apparent on occasions throughout the war, was the frequent use of black numerals, outlined in either white or red; and yellow for the third *Staffeln* - 3, 6 and 9.

Other exceptions to the rules, include the use of brown numerals by 6./JG 26, 3./JG 51 and 3./LG 2, with light blue and/or light grey numerals being used by 5./JG 53. It must also be added that the

Left: Bf 109E-4 of *Stab* I/JG 27, flown by *Gruppe* Adjutant *Oblt* Gunther Bode, which crash landed at Mayfield, Sussex on 9 September 1940. Note the white chevron outlined in black. (via P Scott)

3

Above: Bf 109E-3 'yellow 13' of 3./JG 53, flown by *Fw* Walter Schulz, which force-landed at Langney, Sussex on 30 September 1940. Incorrectly illustrated in the past, this aircraft actually featured a yellow fin and rudder with the paint peeling away from the leading and trailing edges rather than a red or green painted outline. The numeral '13' is probably in the lighter yellow, *Gelb* 27. (via Peter Scott)

Left: *Uffz* Werner Machold's Bf 109E-4 'white 15' of 1./JG 2, at Beaumont-le-Roger in August 1940. Note the modified fuselage cross, 'Bonzo Dog' *Staffel* badge, 'Script R' *Geschwader* shield, and stippled fuselage mottle. (M W Payne Collection)

use of a single letter, (rather than a numeral), appears to have been confined to 4, 5 and 6, (ie II *Gruppe*) LG 2, who also marked their aircraft with a black equilateral triangle, invariably outlined in white. LG 2 had previously been equipped with Henschel Hs 123s in the *Schlacht* (ground attack) role in the Polish Campaign, and when the unit was re-equipped with Bf 109Es retained the marking - in front of the fuselage cross, with the letter in the *Staffel* colour, aft of the cross. *Stab* machines carried green coloured letters aft of the cross - an example being *Oberleutnant* Krafft's green 'D' of *Stab* II/(S)LG 2. I/LG 2 appear to have retained the normal *Staffel* numeral system.

It had also not been uncommon for the *Staffelkapitan* to pilot the aircraft marked with the numeral '1', although by July/August this practice tended to be the exception rather than the rule, as did the practice for the *Staffelkapitan* to carry a metal pennant from the aircraft's radio mast, painted in the *Staffel* colour, another feature which declined during the course of the Battle of Britain.

Another point worthy of mention, is that *Staffel* numerals rarely exceeded the number '16' - aircraft bearing higher numbers tended to indicate that they belonged to a Training *Staffel*.

The different *Gruppen* within a *Geschwader* were identified by a 'symbol' aft of the fuselage cross, invariably in the

Below: *Oblt* Josef 'Pips' Priller's Bf 109E-3, (*W.Nr* 5057) 'yellow 1' of 6./JG 51, when based at Mardyck, Belgium in October 1940. Note Priller's personal emblem, the Ace of Hearts with the words 'Jutta', below the cockpit and 'kill' markings across fin. (Joachim Prien via M W Payne)

same *Staffel* colour(s) as the numerals - exceptions to this being where second *Staffel* aircraft had been re-marked with black numerals and had the *Gruppe* symbol left in the original red.

Stab, (Staff Flight) aircraft used a slightly different system of identification, and the aircraft of these staff pilots and fighter leaders carried distinctive markings for quick identification. Chevron, bar and/or circle markings were carried infront of the fuselage cross instead of numerals, to denote a particular *Stab* rank, which actually varied

Frönhofer's 'yellow 10' of *Stab* III/JG 26).

Both *Gruppe* and *Geschwader Stab* markings were usually painted in black with white trim, or white with black trim, but other examples have also been recorded. *Geschwaderstab* aircraft were not allocated any unit i/d markings aft of the fuselage cross, (as they were not directly attached to any particular *Gruppe*), but some, such as JG 2 *Geschwader Kommodore Major* Helmut Wick's Bf 109E-4, *Werke Nummer* 5344, (in which he lost his life on 28 November 1940), and JG 26 *Geschwader*

Above: A well-known photograph of an aircraft that has also been incorrectly illustrated previously - the Bf 109E-4 of *Oblt* Franz von Werra, *Gruppe* Adjutant of *Stab* II/JG 3, who force-landed at Love's Farm, Marden, Kent on 5 September 1940. The RAF Crash Report stated "wing tips and rudder painted white, fuselage all blue, spinner divided into alternate black and white sections". (Kent Messenger)

Kommodore Major Adolph Galland's E-4, (*W.Nr* 5819), also used circa October/November 1940, were seen with a horizontal bar aft of their fuselage crosses. However, these were almost certainly part of both commanders' interpretation of their *Geschwader Kommodore's Stab* rank markings, rather than a III *Gruppe* symbol, as both aircraft were also marked with a single chevron and horizontal bar infront of the fuslage cross, instead of the double-chevron and bar which was the original pre-war marking for a *Geschwader Kommodore*.

As a means of developing *esprit de corps*, aircraft were further frequently embellished by both personal 'artwork' and unit badges and, to a lesser extent by names. Not all the unit badges were

somewhat between units. Fig 3 shows some general styles, but others will be found from examination of the profiles. As mentioned earlier, not all *Stab* personnel were actually pilots, and it was presumably in such cases where their was insufficient *Stab* personnel able to fly, that 'normal' *Staffel* pilots were picked to fly with the *Stabsschwarm*, in numeral-marked aircraft, (eg *Oblt* Wilhelm

Above: Bf 109Es of 9./JG 2 at Oye-Plage east of Calais at the end of August 1940. Note the yellow cowlings with the *Stechmücke* (insect) *Staffel* badge.

Right: 7./JG 2 cowlings and spinners being painted with the yellow tactical paint, and having the Staffel badge stencilled on. Note the III Gruppe Adjutant's aircraft in the background.

Messerschmitt Bf 109E Camouflage and Markings - 1940

02 grau	04 gelb	21 weiss	22 schwarz	23 rot	24 dunkelblau	25 hellgrun	26 brun
27 gelb	65 hellblau	70 schwartzgrun	71 dunkelgrun	74 graugrun	75 mittelgrau	76 hellgrau	light blue

Messerschmitt Bf 109E-1 of 2./JG1, based at Vorden, Germany, in January 1940.

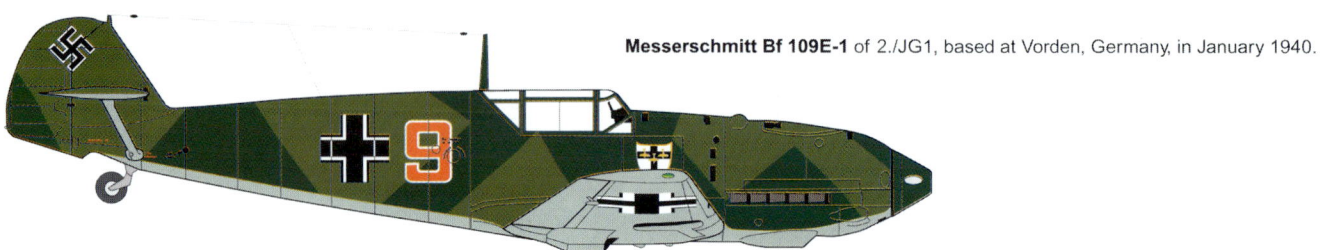

Messerschmitt Bf 109E-1 of Stab /JG2, based at Frankfurt-Rebstock, Germany, in January 1940. Pilot Oberst Gerd von Massow, Geschwader Kommodore.

Messerschmitt Bf 109E-1 of 3./JG2, based at Frankfurt-Rebstock, Germany, in January 1940.

Messerschmitt Bf 109E-1 of 2./JG76, based at Frankfurt-am-Main, Germany, in January 1940. Pilot Obgef. Milde.

Messerschmitt Bf 109E-3 of 1./JG26, based at Diepholz, Germany, in February 1940. Pilot Lt. Eberhard Henrici.

Messerschmitt Bf 109E-1 of 2./JG26, based at Werl, Germany, in March 1940. Pilot Oblt. Fritz Losigkeit, Staffelkapitan.

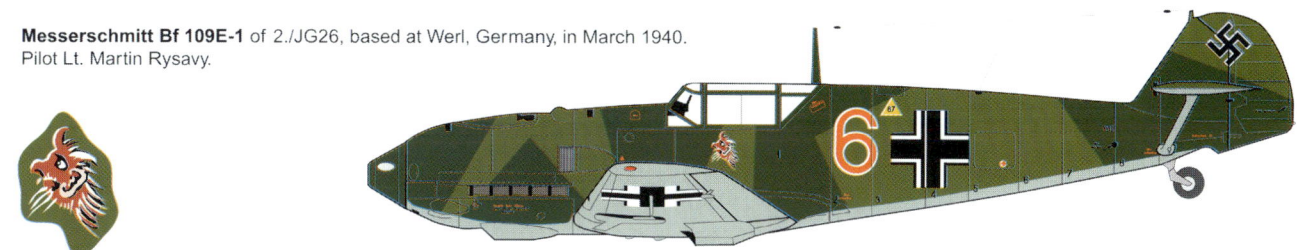
Messerschmitt Bf 109E-1 of 2./JG26, based at Werl, Germany, in March 1940. Pilot Lt. Martin Rysavy.

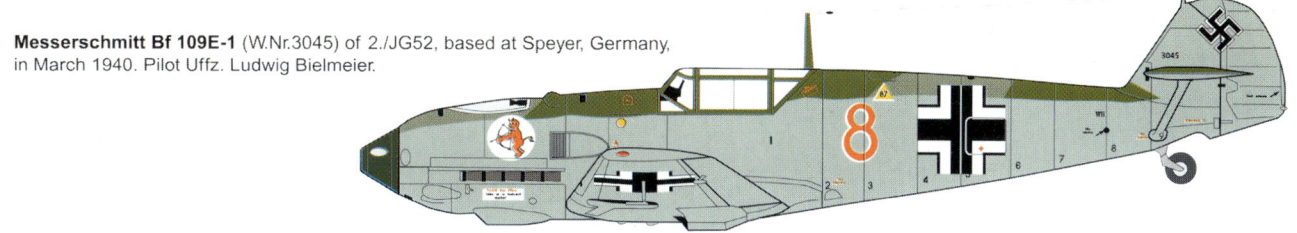
Messerschmitt Bf 109E-1 (W.Nr.3045) of 2./JG52, based at Speyer, Germany, in March 1940. Pilot Uffz. Ludwig Bielmeier.

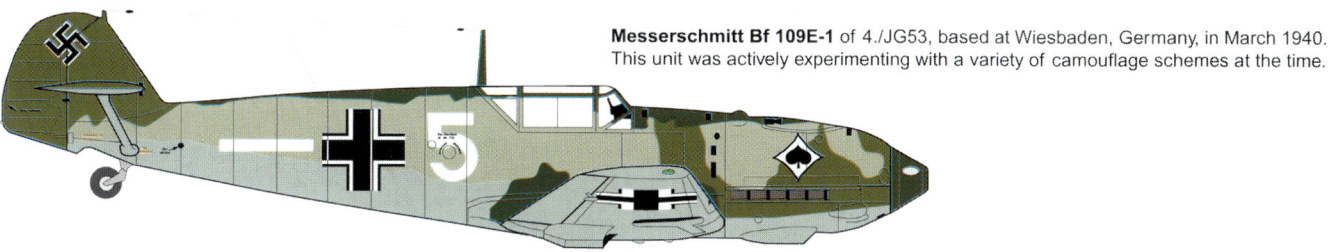
Messerschmitt Bf 109E-1 of 4./JG53, based at Wiesbaden, Germany, in March 1940. This unit was actively experimenting with a variety of camouflage schemes at the time.

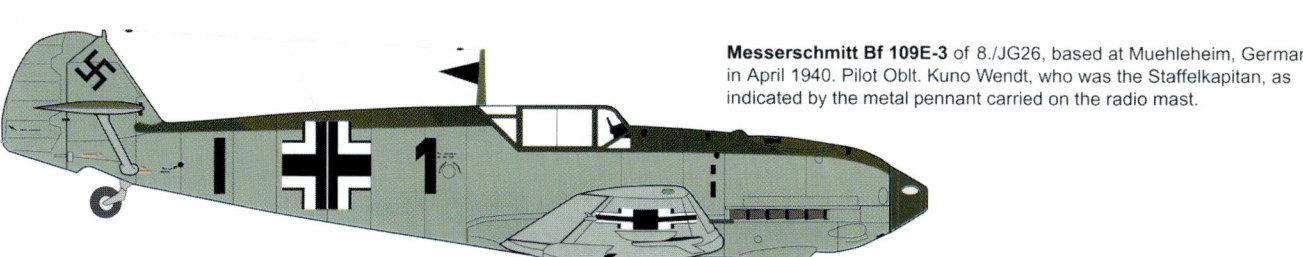
Messerschmitt Bf 109E-3 of 8./JG26, based at Muehleheim, Germany, in April 1940. Pilot Oblt. Kuno Wendt, who was the Staffelkapitan, as indicated by the metal pennant carried on the radio mast.

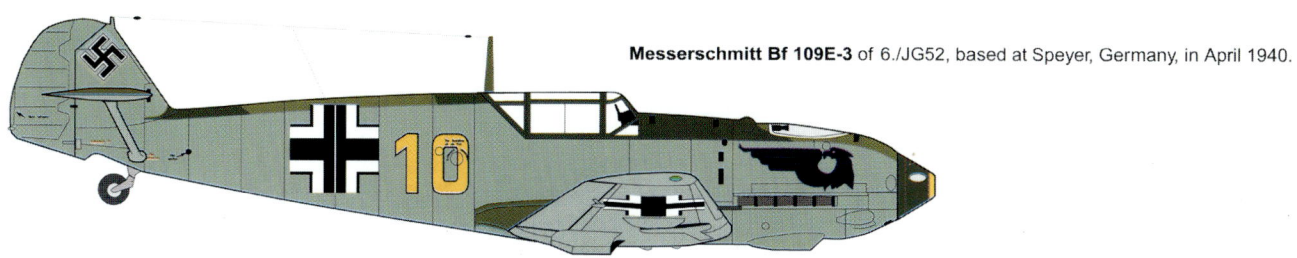
Messerschmitt Bf 109E-3 of 6./JG52, based at Speyer, Germany, in April 1940.

7

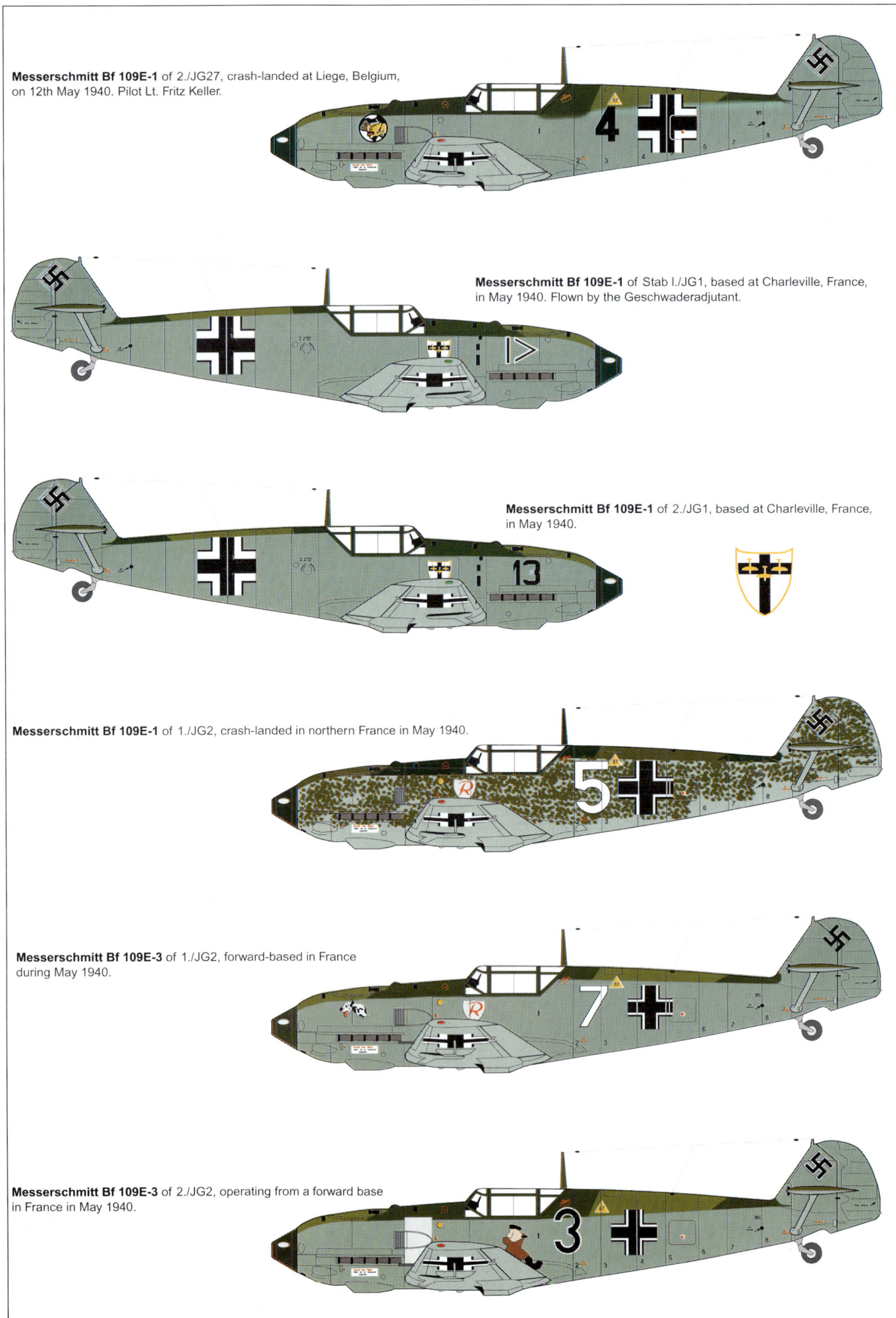

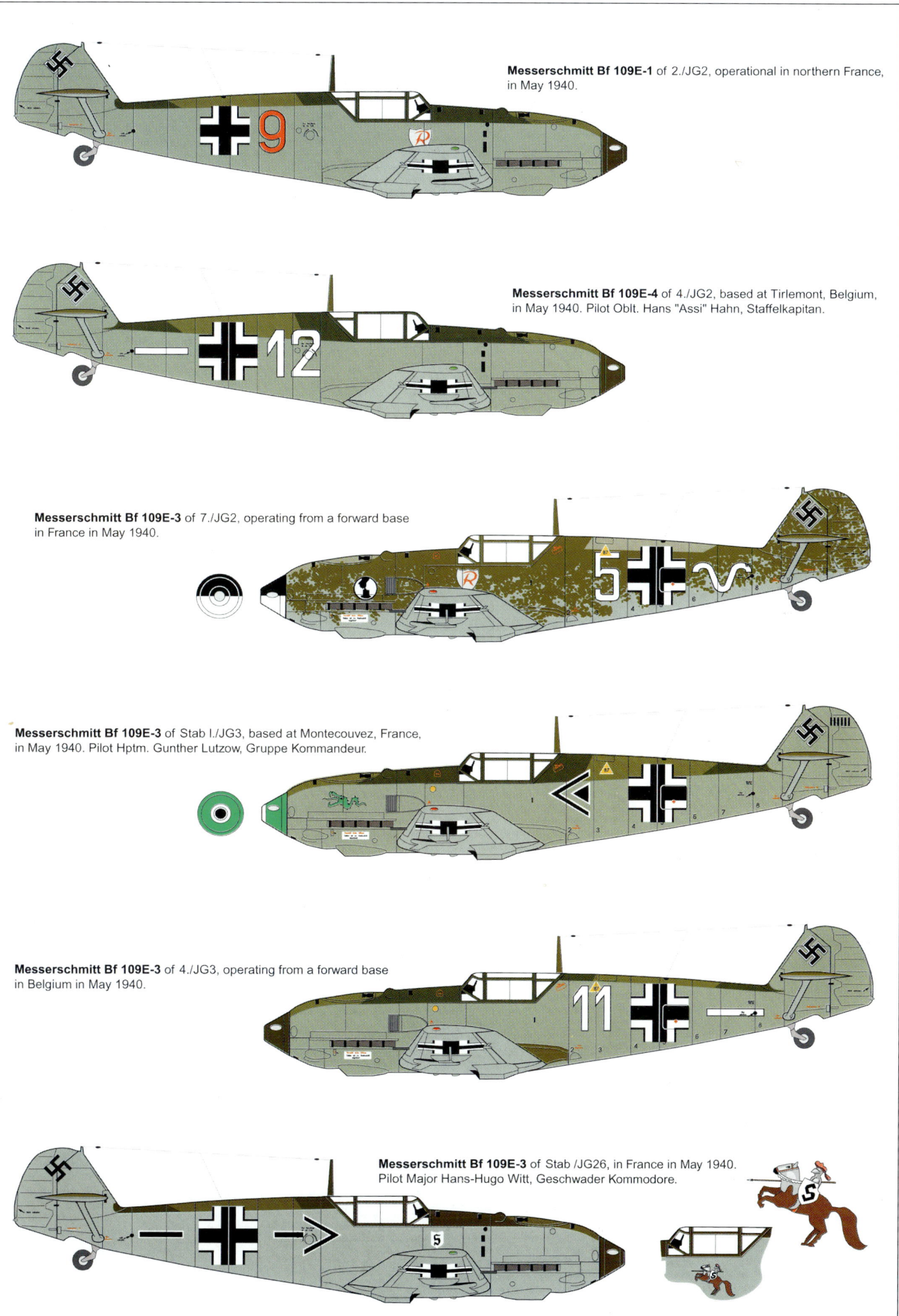

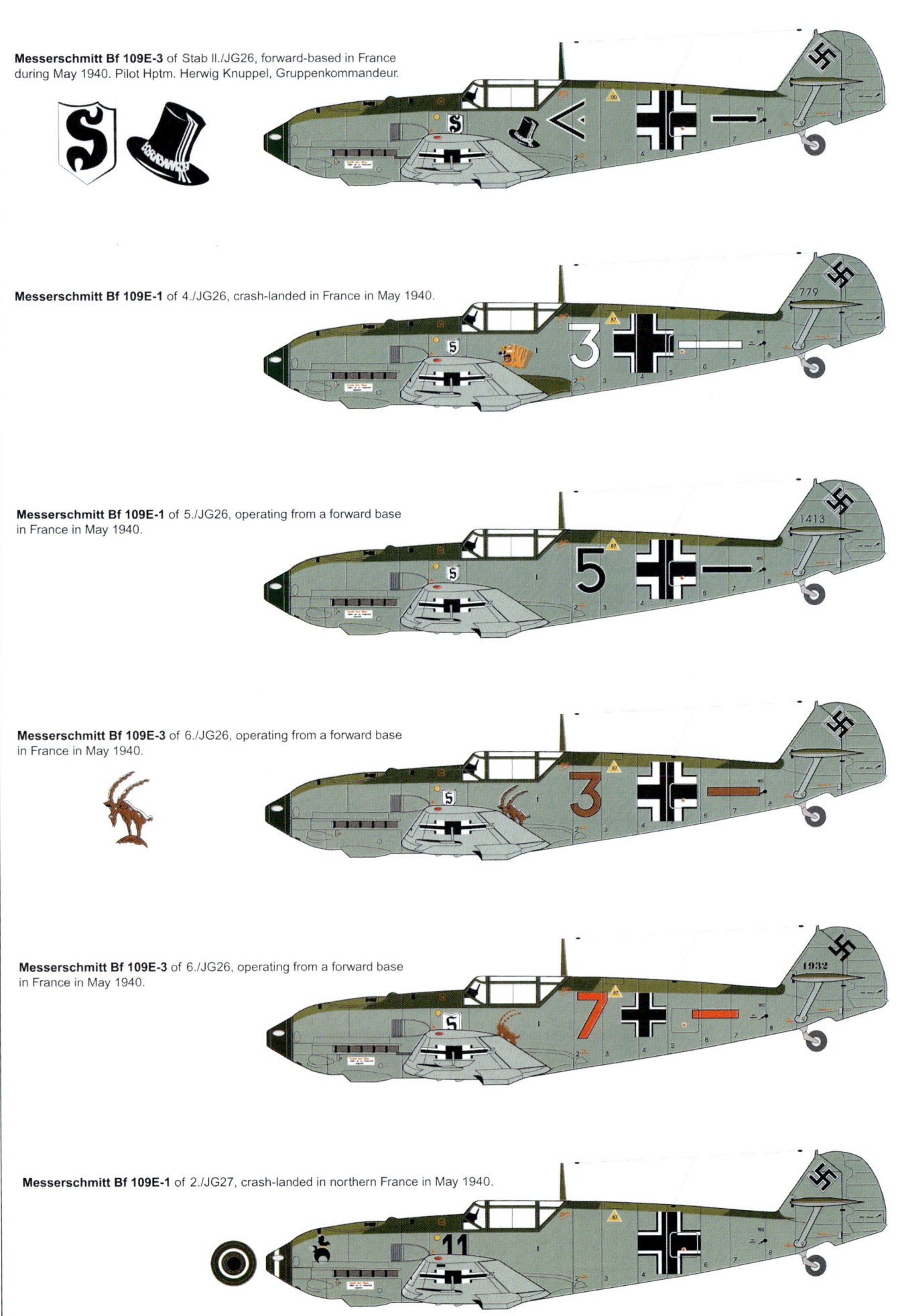

Messerschmitt Bf 109E-3 of Stab II./JG26, forward-based in France during May 1940. Pilot Hptm. Herwig Knuppel, Gruppenkommandeur.

Messerschmitt Bf 109E-1 of 4./JG26, crash-landed in France in May 1940.

Messerschmitt Bf 109E-1 of 5./JG26, operating from a forward base in France in May 1940.

Messerschmitt Bf 109E-3 of 6./JG26, operating from a forward base in France in May 1940.

Messerschmitt Bf 109E-3 of 6./JG26, operating from a forward base in France in May 1940.

Messerschmitt Bf 109E-1 of 2./JG27, crash-landed in northern France in May 1940.

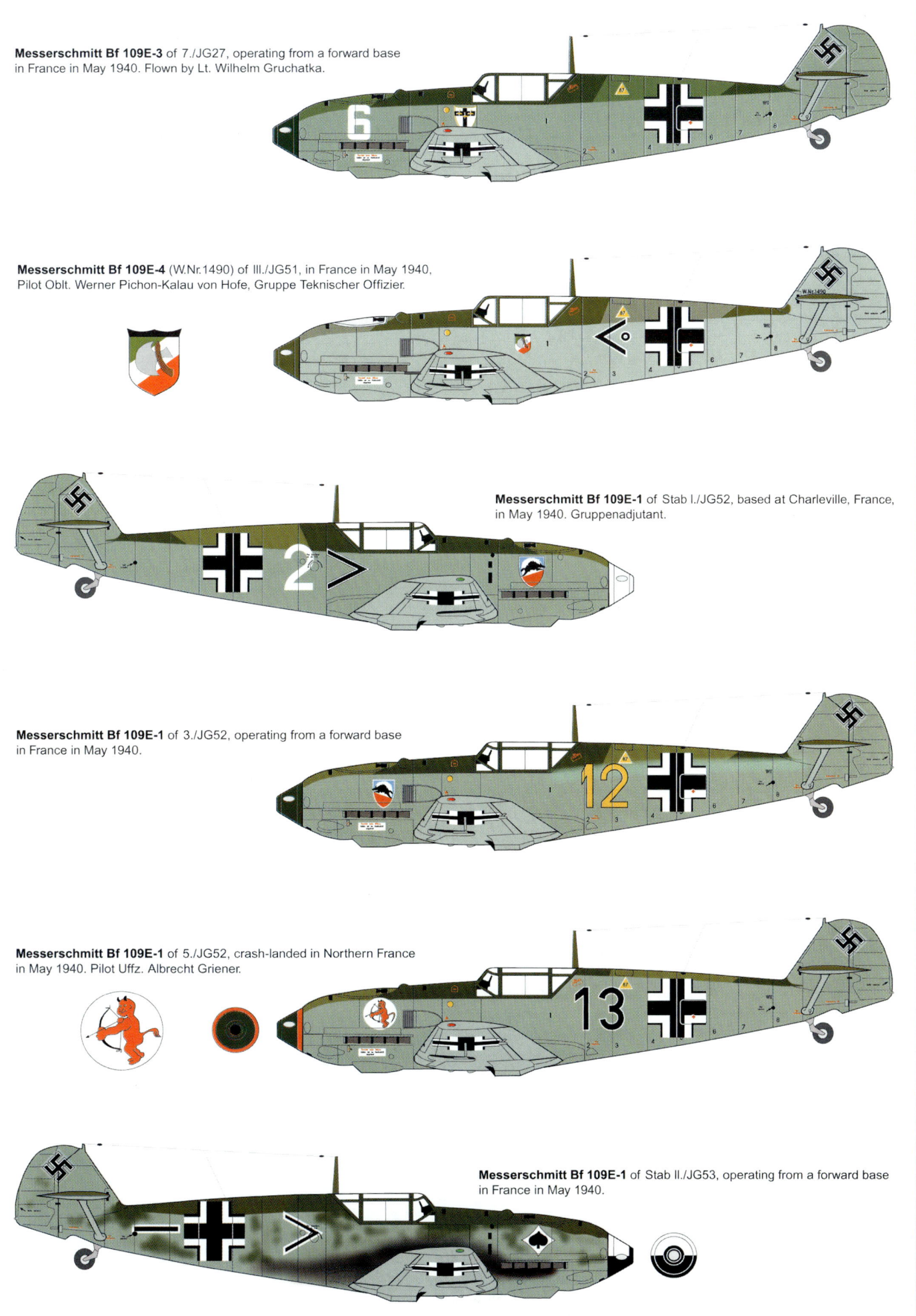

Messerschmitt Bf 109E-3 of Stab III./JG53, based at Lors, France, in May 1940. Pilot Hptm. Werner Molders, Gruppenkommodore.

Messerschmitt Bf 109E-3 of Stab I./JG77, based at Aalborg, Denmark, in May 1940. Pilot Oblt. Kunze, Gruppenadjutant.

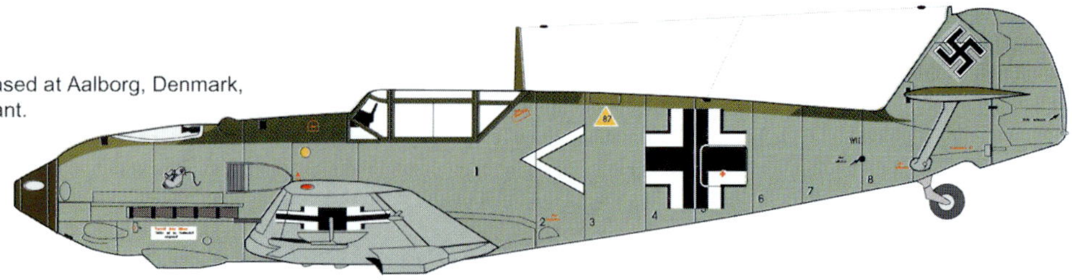

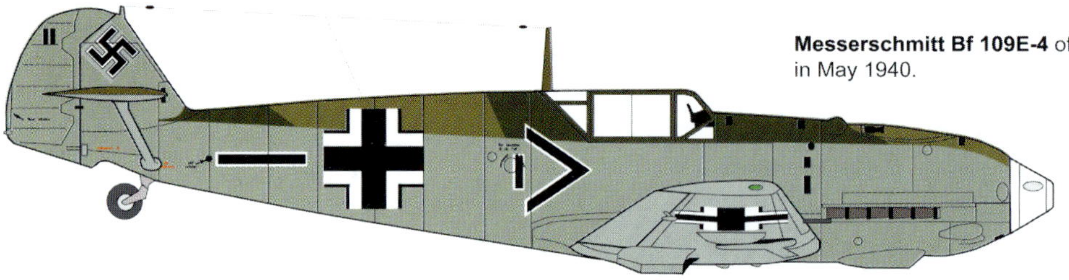

Messerschmitt Bf 109E-4 of Stab II./JG77, based at Kristiansand, Norway, in May 1940.

Messerschmitt Bf 109E-4 of Stab III./JG52, crash-landed at Roye, France on 21st May 1940. Pilot Major Dr. Erich Mix, Gruppenkommandeur.

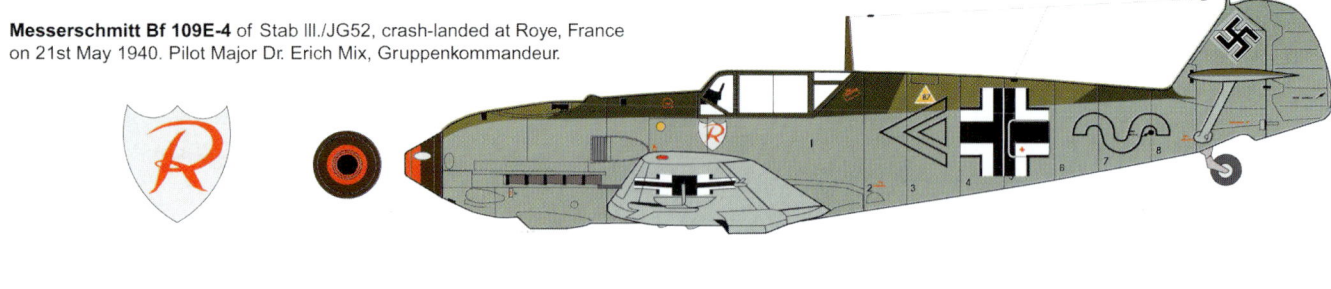

Messerschmitt Bf 109E-3 of 1/JG2, crash-landed in northern France on 26th. May 1940. Pilot Oblt. Otto Bertram.

Messerschmitt Bf 109E-1 (W.Nr.3247) of 4./JG54 which, following an air test, was mistakenly landed at the Armee de l'Aire base of Orconte, France, on 30th May 1940. Pilot Uffz. Hager was taken prisoner.

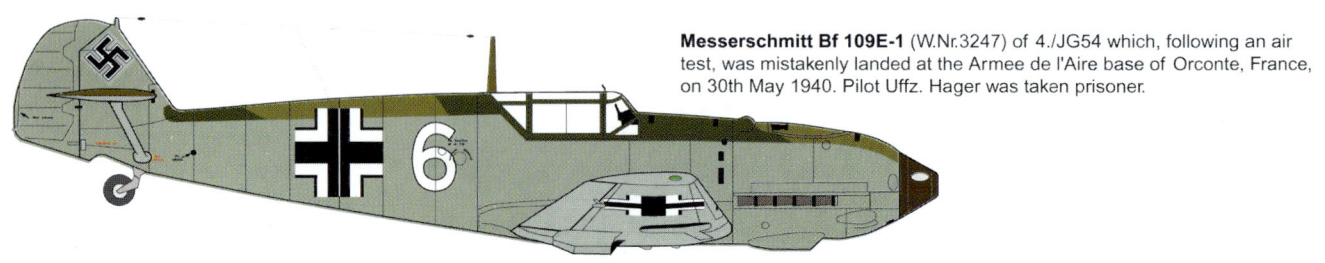

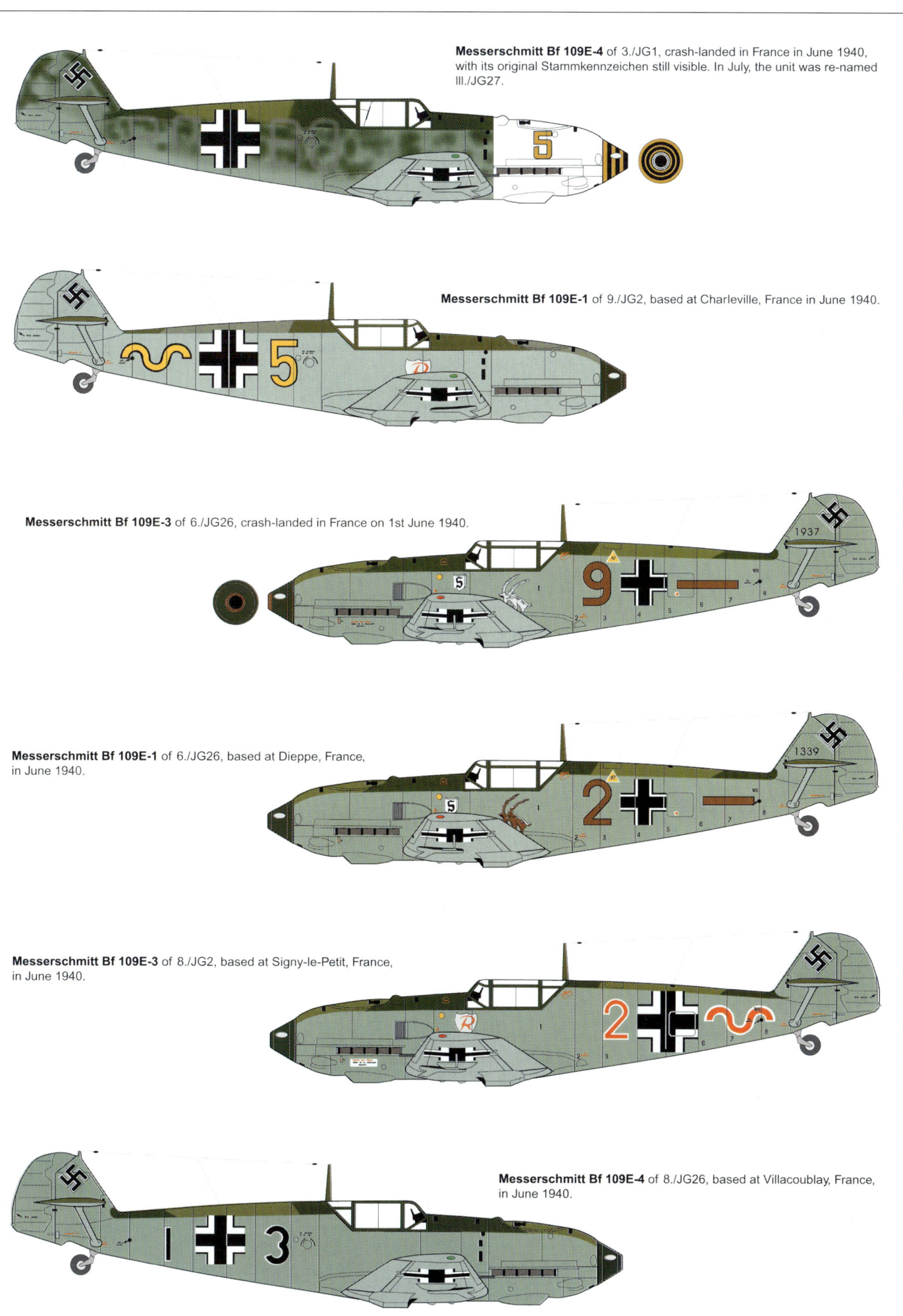

Messerschmitt Bf 109E-4 of 8./JG26, based at Villacoublay, France, in June 1940.

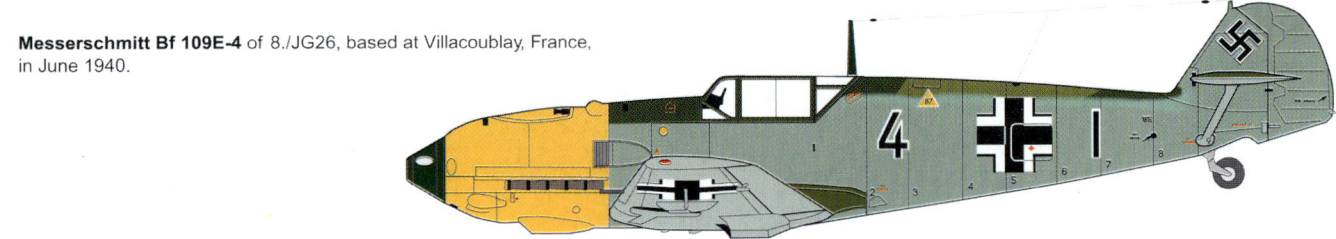

Messerschmitt Bf 109E-1 of 1./JG53, in France in June 1940. Pilot Hpt. Werner Molders, Gruppenkommandeur.

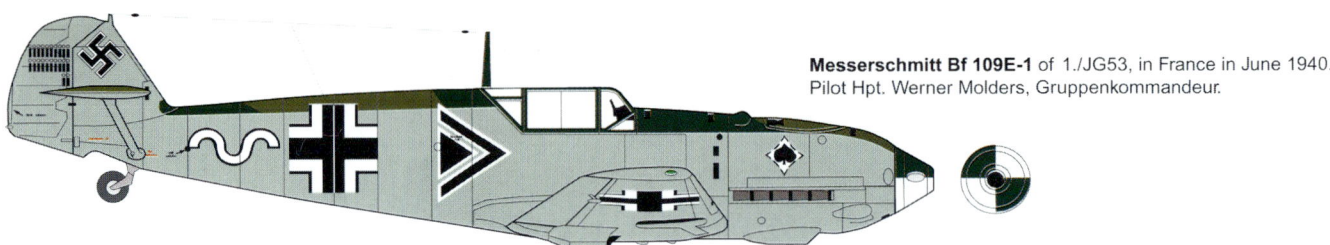

Messerschmitt Bf 109E-1 of 6./JG53, based at Charleville, France, in June 1940.

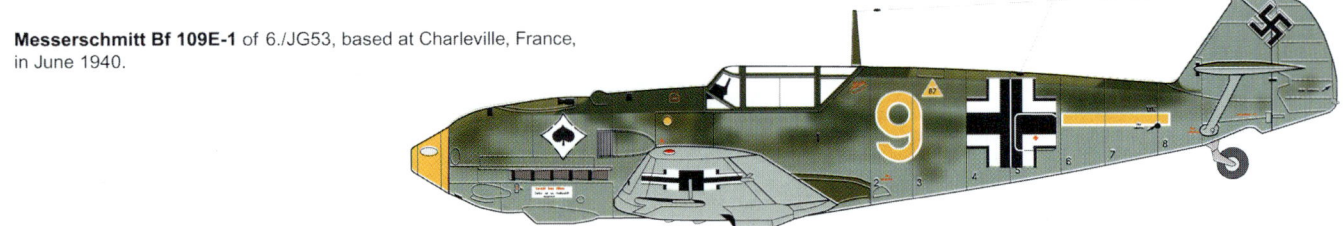

Messerschmitt Bf 109E-1 of 2./JG76, which was attached to JG2 throughout the French campaign, crash-landed in northern France in June 1940.

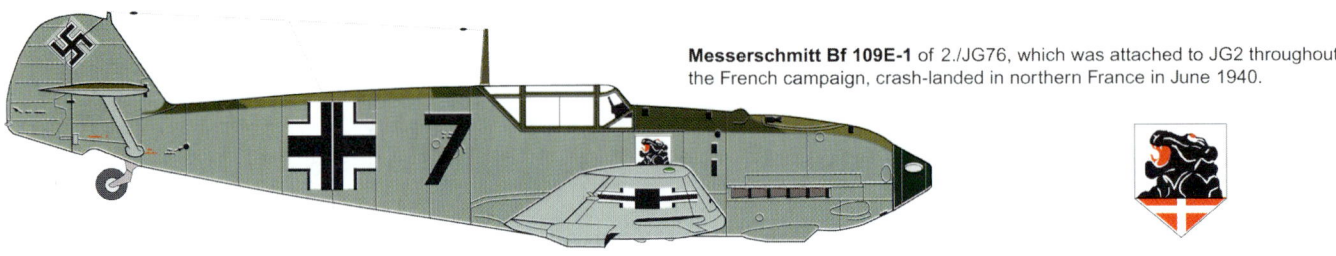

Messerschmitt Bf 109E-1 of 4./JG77, based at Vaernes, Norway, in June 1940.

Messerschmitt Bf 109E-1 of 6./JG77, based at Vaernes, Norway, in June 1940. Pilot Ofw. Kurt Ubben. The fresh paintwork beneath the cockpit covered a witch on a broomstick.

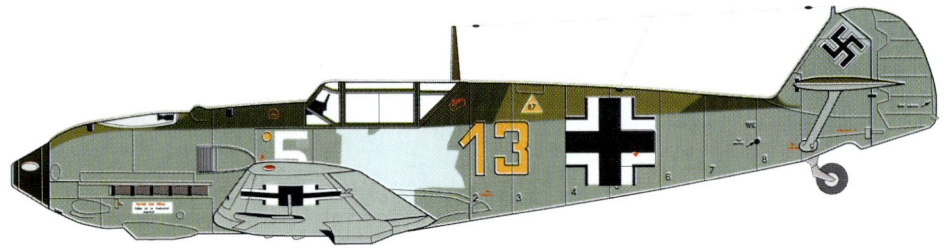

14

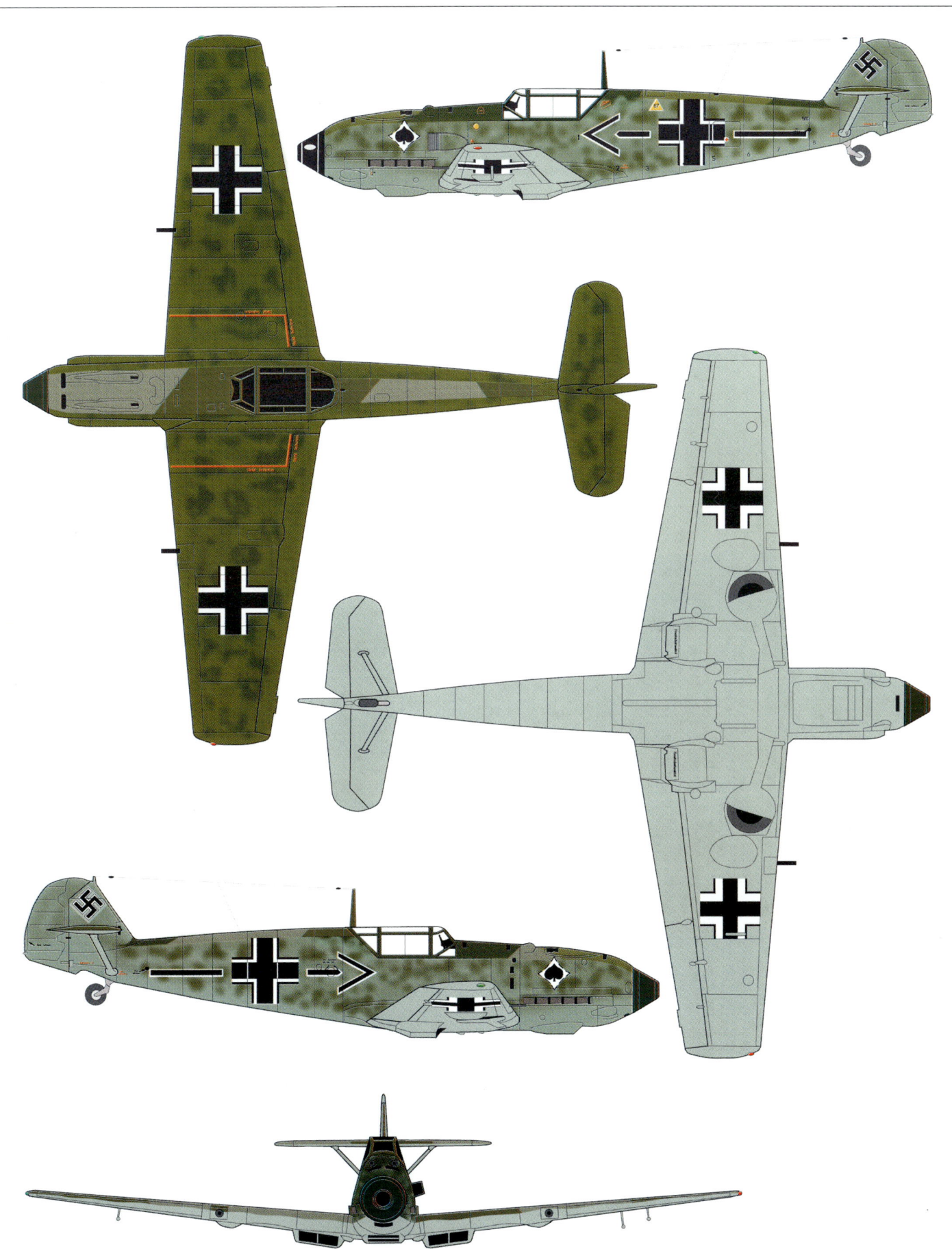

Messerschmitt Bf 109E-4 of Stab./JG53, in France in June 1940. Its pilot was Major Hans-Jurgen von Cramon-Taubadel, the Geschwader Kommodore. he incurred the wrath of Hermann Goering by marrying into a Jewish family. As a consequence, Goering apparently ordered the overpainting of the "Pik-As" device by a red band on all of the unit aircraft. Some of the pilots reacted by overpainting their aircraft's swastika. By no means all aircraft were affected, as will be evident from later profiles, particularly of those machines which crashed in England still with the ace still visible. upon the appointment of a new Kommodore, the "Pik-As" re-appeared officially.

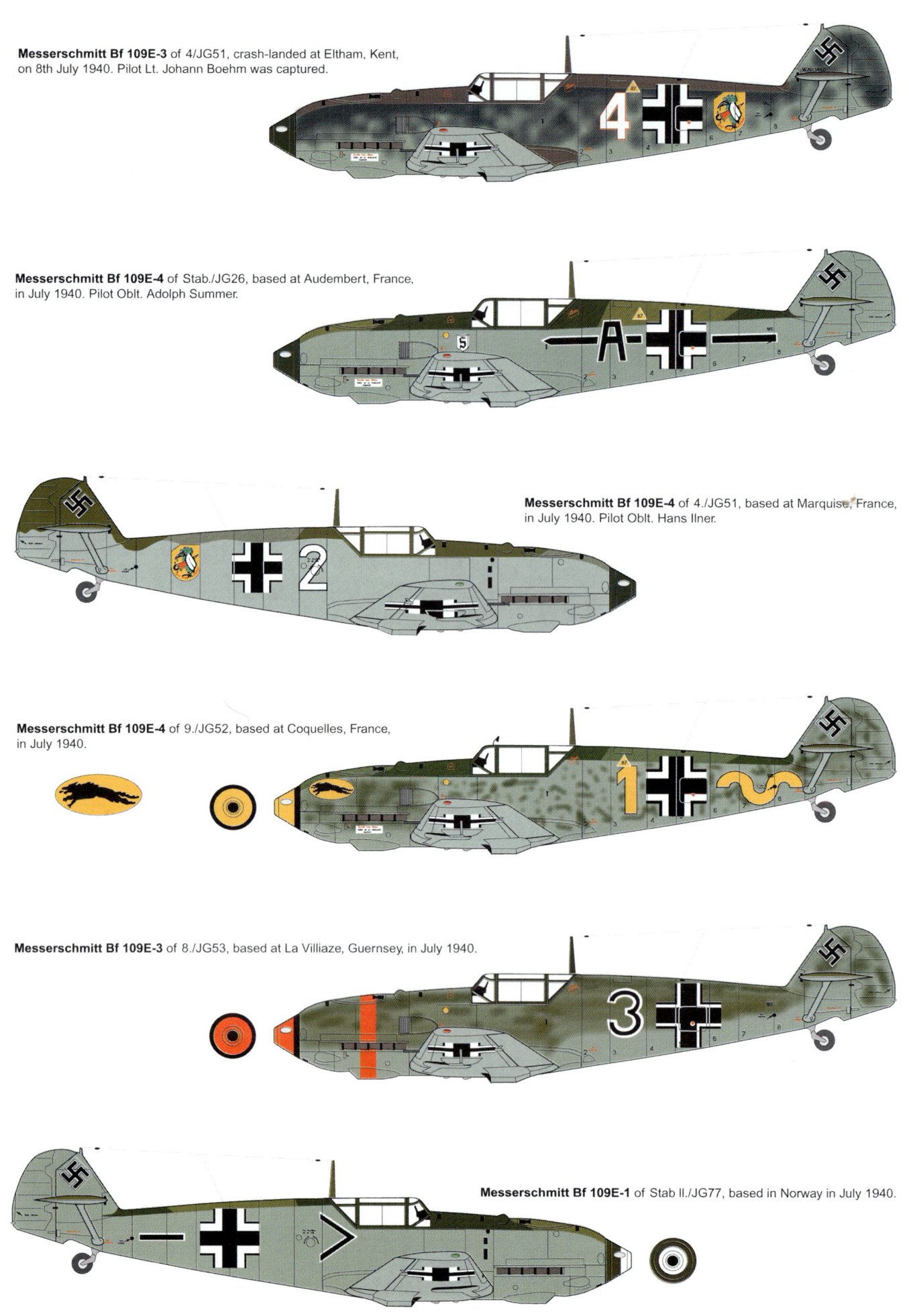

Messerschmitt Bf 109E-3 of 4./JG51, crash-landed at Eltham, Kent, on 8th July 1940. Pilot Lt. Johann Boehm was captured.

Messerschmitt Bf 109E-4 of Stab./JG26, based at Audembert, France, in July 1940. Pilot Oblt. Adolph Summer.

Messerschmitt Bf 109E-4 of 4./JG51, based at Marquise, France, in July 1940. Pilot Oblt. Hans Ilner.

Messerschmitt Bf 109E-4 of 9./JG52, based at Coquelles, France, in July 1940.

Messerschmitt Bf 109E-3 of 8./JG53, based at La Villiaze, Guernsey, in July 1940.

Messerschmitt Bf 109E-1 of Stab II./JG77, based in Norway in July 1940.

16

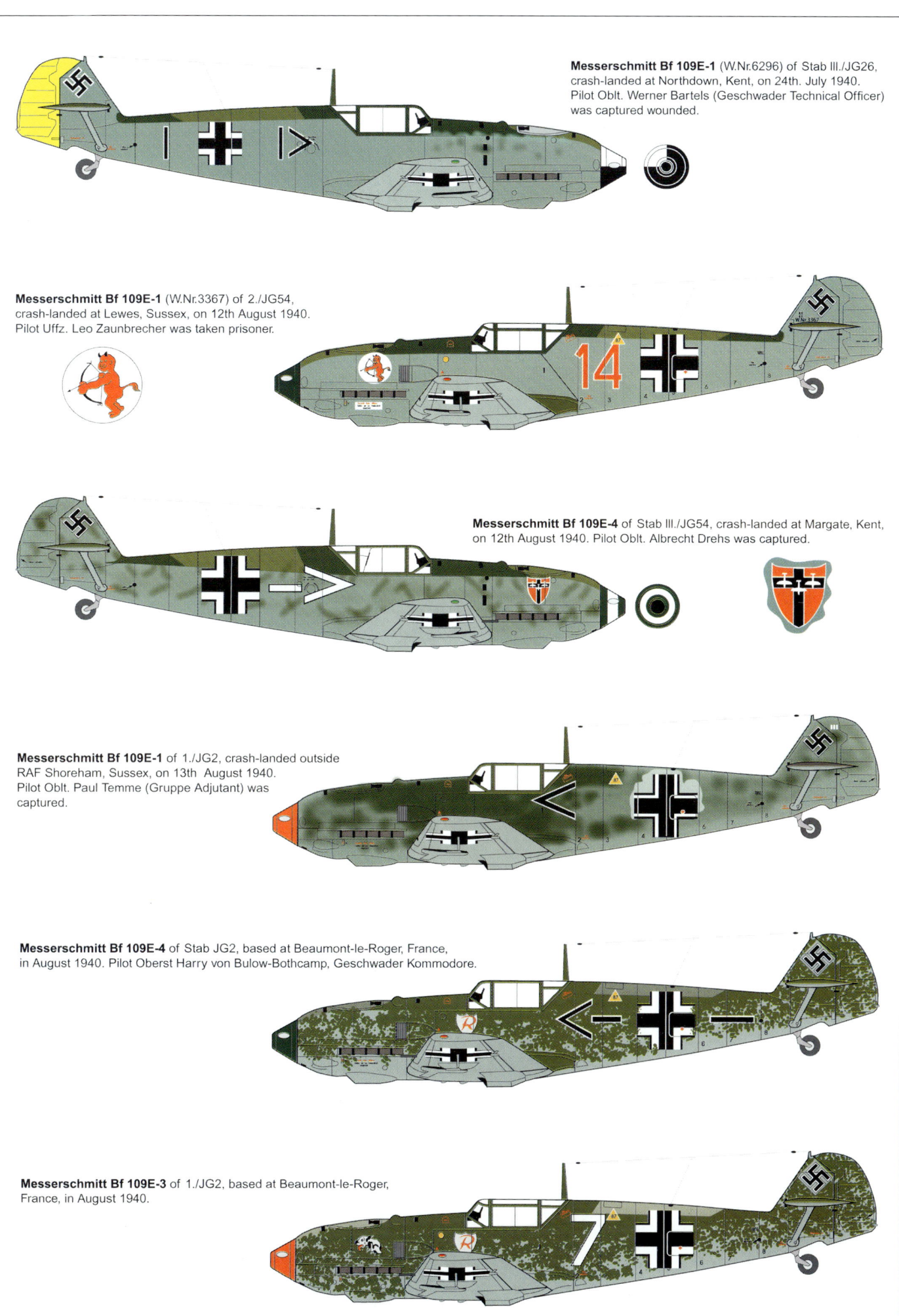

Messerschmitt Bf 109E-1 (W.Nr.6296) of Stab III./JG26, crash-landed at Northdown, Kent, on 24th. July 1940. Pilot Oblt. Werner Bartels (Geschwader Technical Officer) was captured wounded.

Messerschmitt Bf 109E-1 (W.Nr.3367) of 2./JG54, crash-landed at Lewes, Sussex, on 12th August 1940. Pilot Uffz. Leo Zaunbrecher was taken prisoner.

Messerschmitt Bf 109E-4 of Stab III./JG54, crash-landed at Margate, Kent, on 12th August 1940. Pilot Oblt. Albrecht Drehs was captured.

Messerschmitt Bf 109E-1 of 1./JG2, crash-landed outside RAF Shoreham, Sussex, on 13th August 1940. Pilot Oblt. Paul Temme (Gruppe Adjutant) was captured.

Messerschmitt Bf 109E-4 of Stab JG2, based at Beaumont-le-Roger, France, in August 1940. Pilot Oberst Harry von Bulow-Bothcamp, Geschwader Kommodore.

Messerschmitt Bf 109E-3 of 1./JG2, based at Beaumont-le-Roger, France, in August 1940.

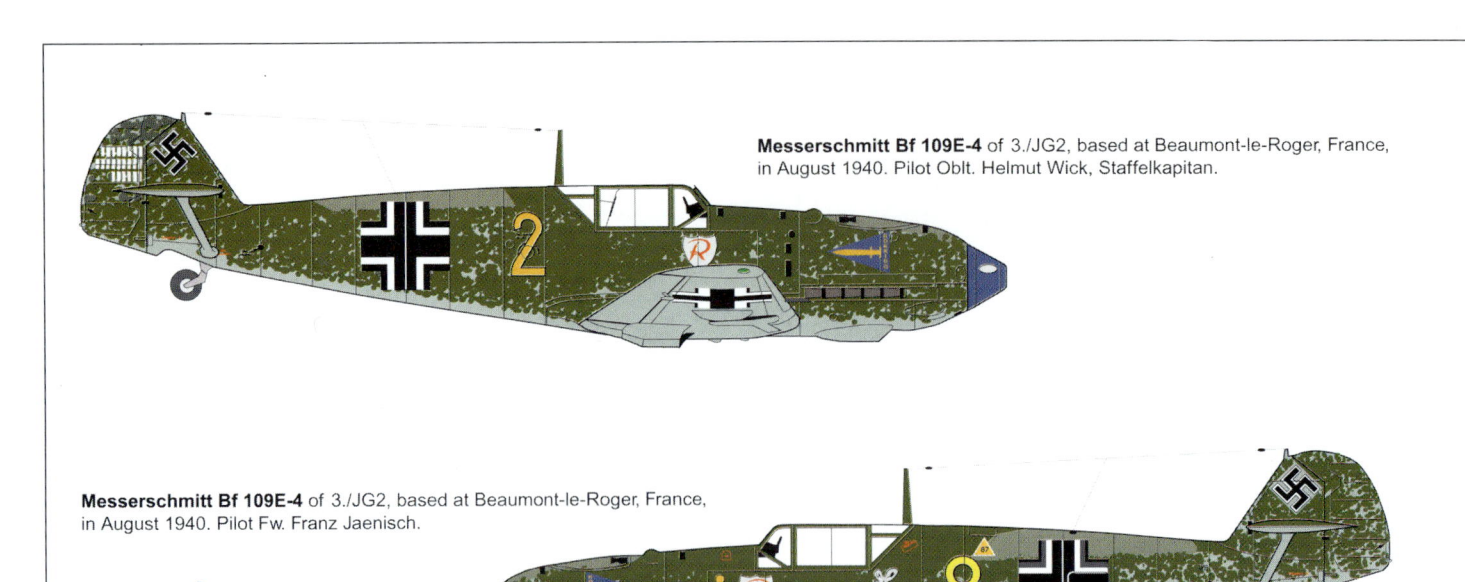

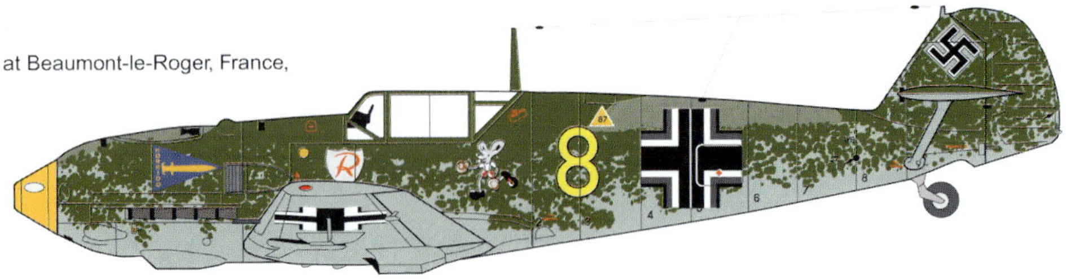

Messerschmitt Bf 109E-4 of 3./JG2, based at Beaumont-le-Roger, France, in August 1940. Pilot Oblt. Helmut Wick, Staffelkapitan.

Messerschmitt Bf 109E-4 of 3./JG2, based at Beaumont-le-Roger, France, in August 1940. Pilot Fw. Franz Jaenisch.

Messerschmitt Bf 109E-4 of 7./JG2, based at Le Havre, France, in August 1940.

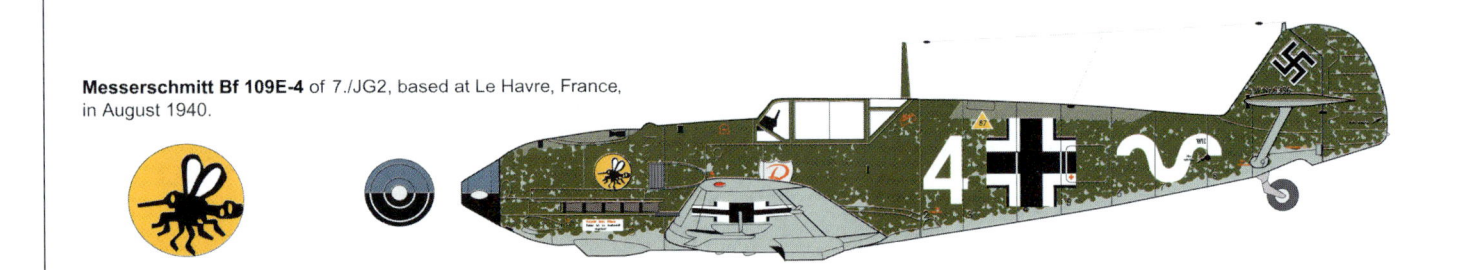

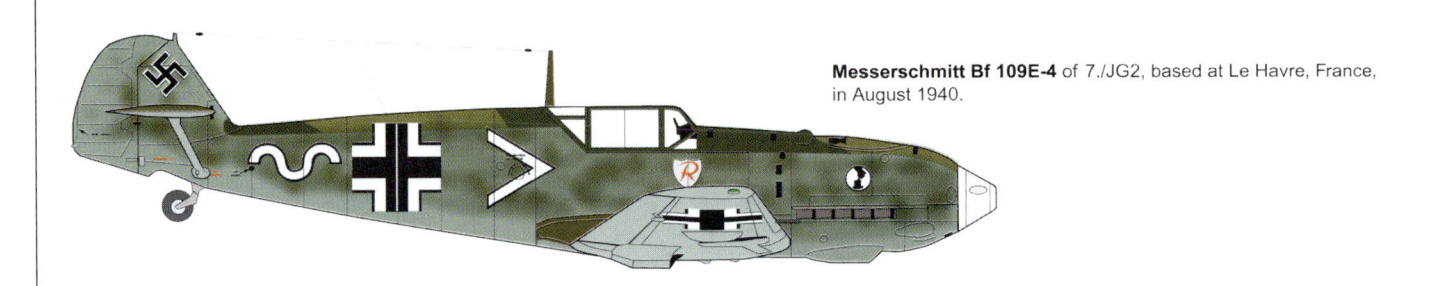

Messerschmitt Bf 109E-4 of 7./JG2, based at Le Havre, France, in August 1940.

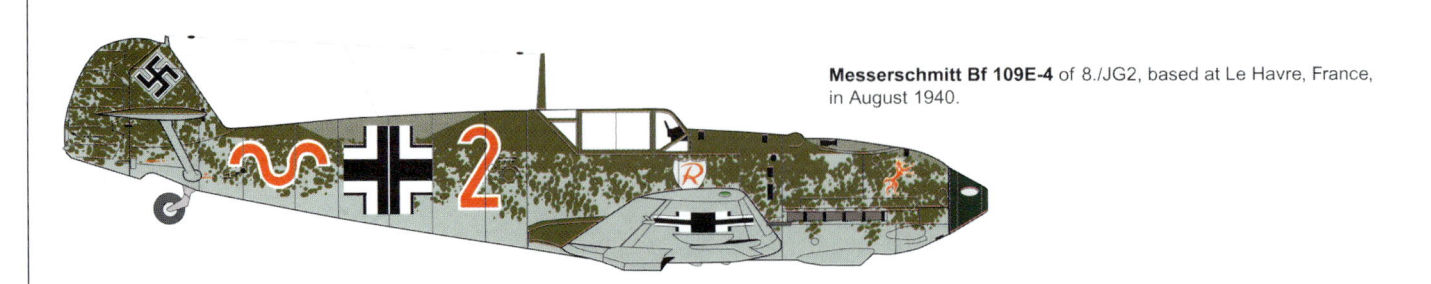

Messerschmitt Bf 109E-4 of 8./JG2, based at Le Havre, France, in August 1940.

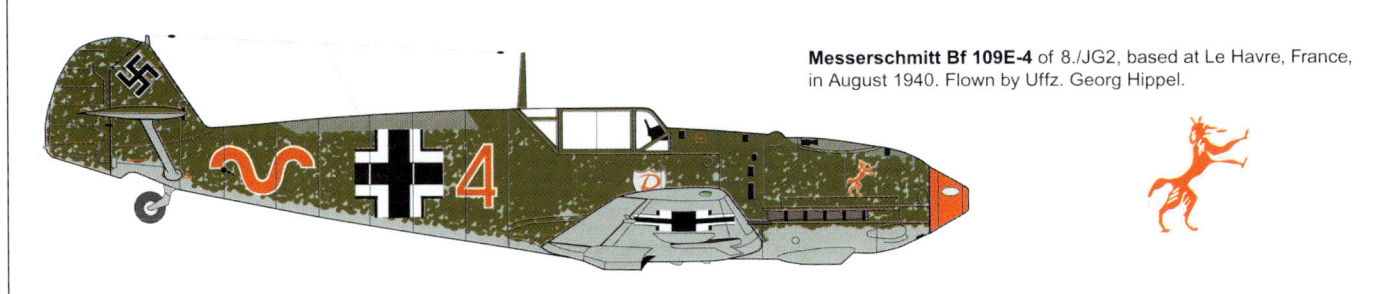

Messerschmitt Bf 109E-4 of 8./JG2, based at Le Havre, France, in August 1940. Flown by Uffz. Georg Hippel.

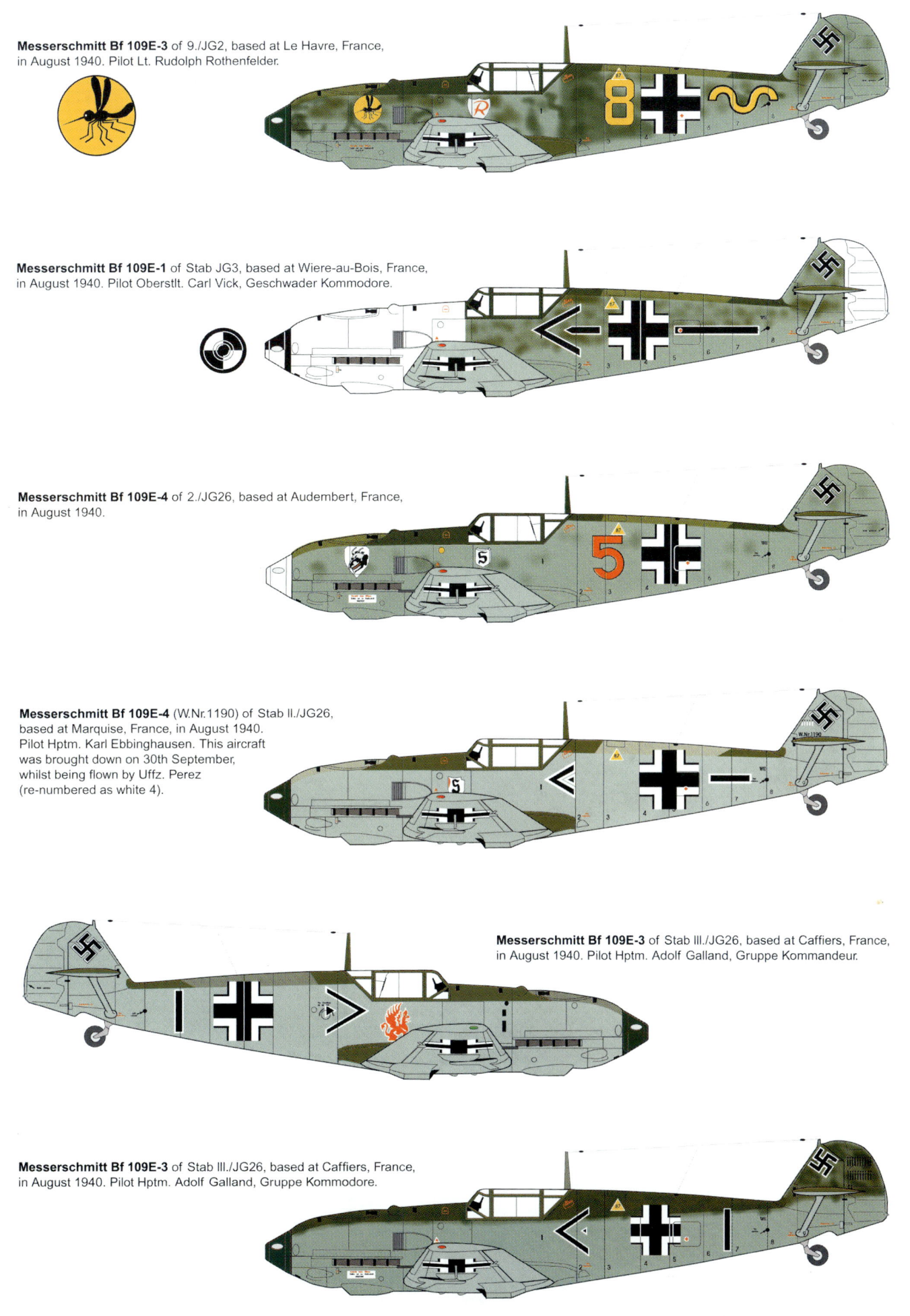

Messerschmitt Bf 109E-3 of 9./JG2, based at Le Havre, France, in August 1940. Pilot Lt. Rudolph Rothenfelder.

Messerschmitt Bf 109E-1 of Stab JG3, based at Wiere-au-Bois, France, in August 1940. Pilot Oberstlt. Carl Vick, Geschwader Kommodore.

Messerschmitt Bf 109E-4 of 2./JG26, based at Audembert, France, in August 1940.

Messerschmitt Bf 109E-4 (W.Nr.1190) of Stab II./JG26, based at Marquise, France, in August 1940. Pilot Hptm. Karl Ebbinghausen. This aircraft was brought down on 30th September, whilst being flown by Uffz. Perez (re-numbered as white 4).

Messerschmitt Bf 109E-3 of Stab III./JG26, based at Caffiers, France, in August 1940. Pilot Hptm. Adolf Galland, Gruppe Kommandeur.

Messerschmitt Bf 109E-3 of Stab III./JG26, based at Caffiers, France, in August 1940. Pilot Hptm. Adolf Galland, Gruppe Kommodore.

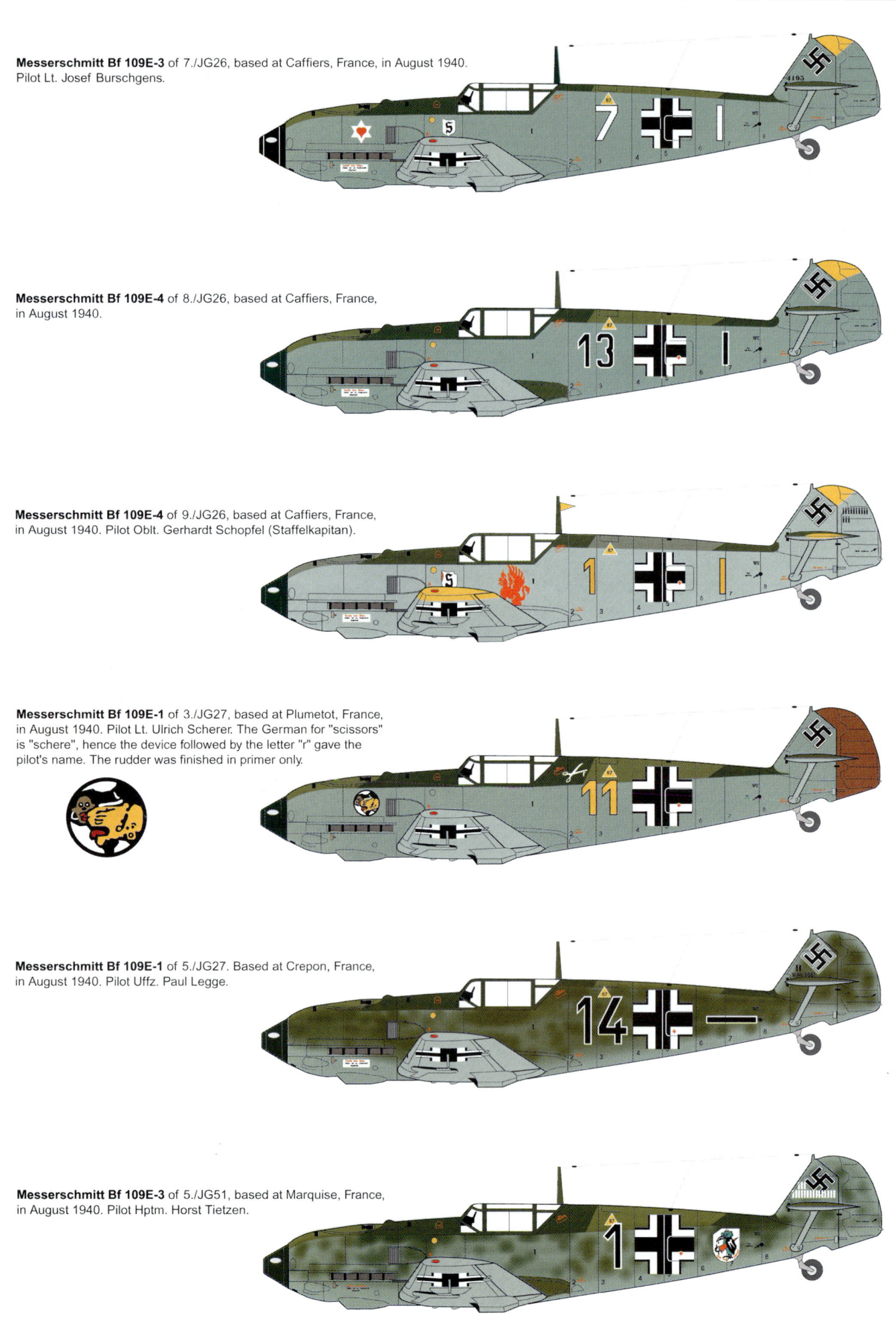

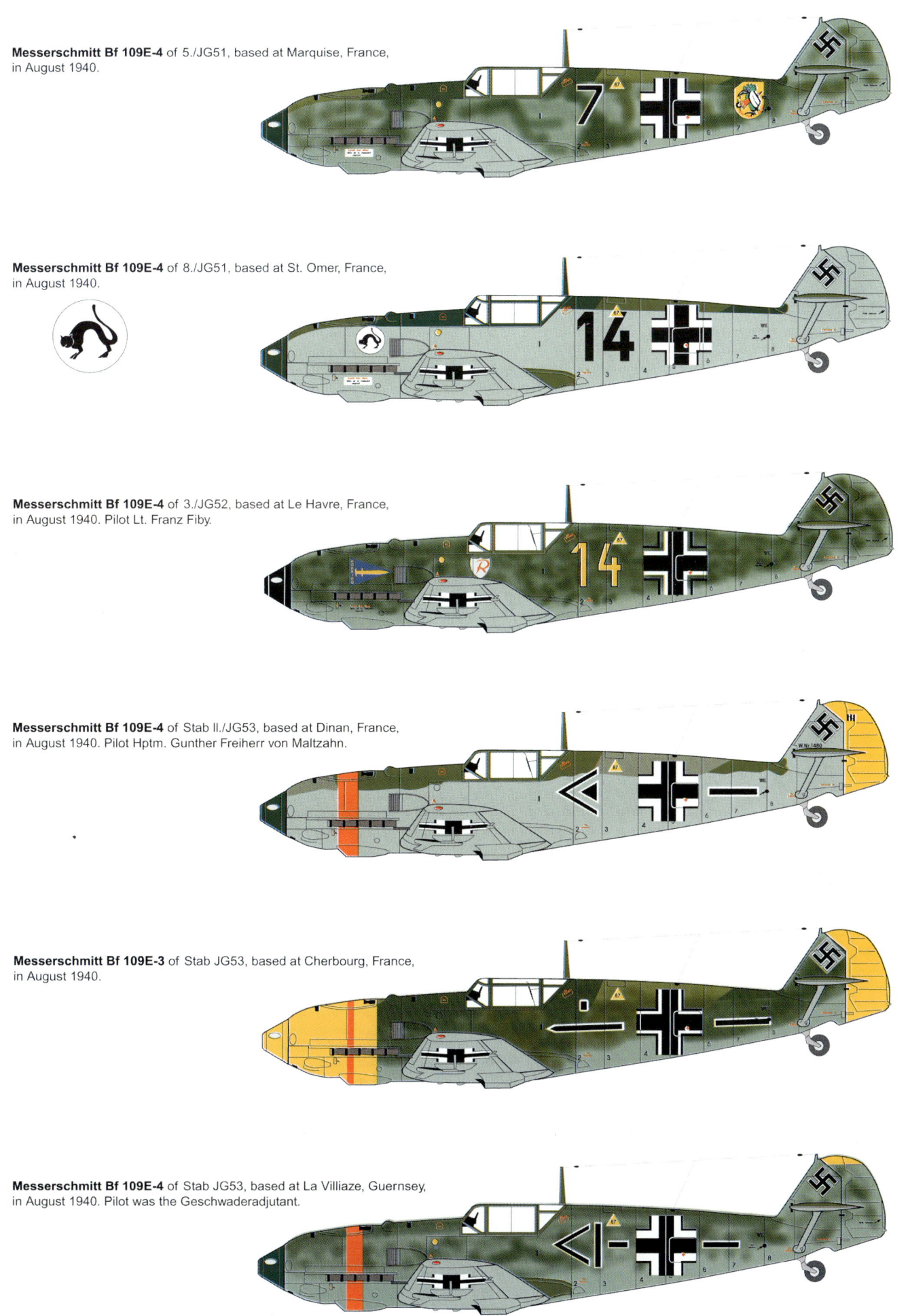

Messerschmitt Bf 109E-4 of 5./JG51, based at Marquise, France, in August 1940.

Messerschmitt Bf 109E-4 of 8./JG51, based at St. Omer, France, in August 1940.

Messerschmitt Bf 109E-4 of 3./JG52, based at Le Havre, France, in August 1940. Pilot Lt. Franz Fiby.

Messerschmitt Bf 109E-4 of Stab II./JG53, based at Dinan, France, in August 1940. Pilot Hptm. Gunther Freiherr von Maltzahn.

Messerschmitt Bf 109E-3 of Stab JG53, based at Cherbourg, France, in August 1940.

Messerschmitt Bf 109E-4 of Stab JG53, based at La Villiaze, Guernsey, in August 1940. Pilot was the Geschwaderadjutant.

21

Messerschmitt Bf 109E-1 of 5./JG53, based at Guernsey, Channel Islands, in August 1940.

Messerschmitt Bf 109E-1 of 6./JG53, based at Dinan, France, in August 1940.

Messerschmitt Bf 109E-3 of 8./JG53, based at Guernsey, Channel Islands, in August 1940.

Messerschmitt Bf 109E-3 of Stab II./JG54, based at Marquise, France, in August 1940.

Messerschmitt Bf 109E-4 of 9./JG54, based at Foret de Guines, France, in August 1940. Pilot Lt. Waldemar Wubke.

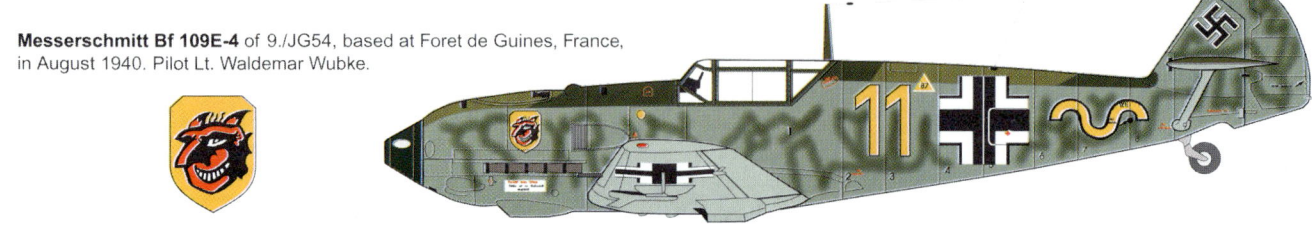

Messerschmitt Bf 109E-4 of 3./LG2, based at Calais-Marck, France, in August 1940.

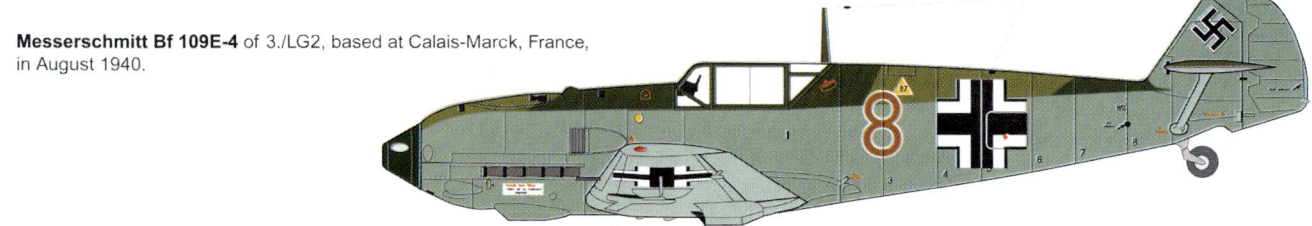

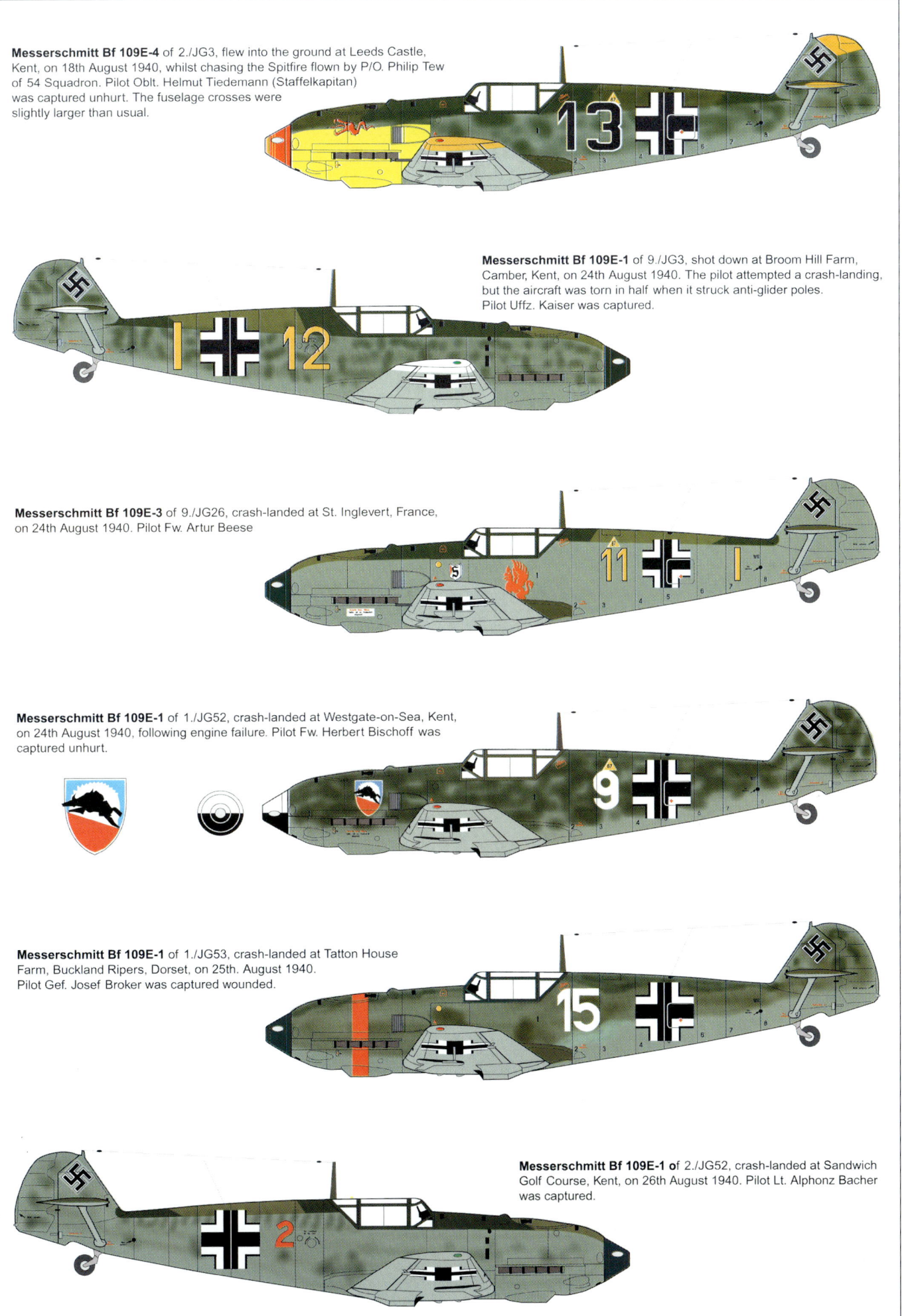

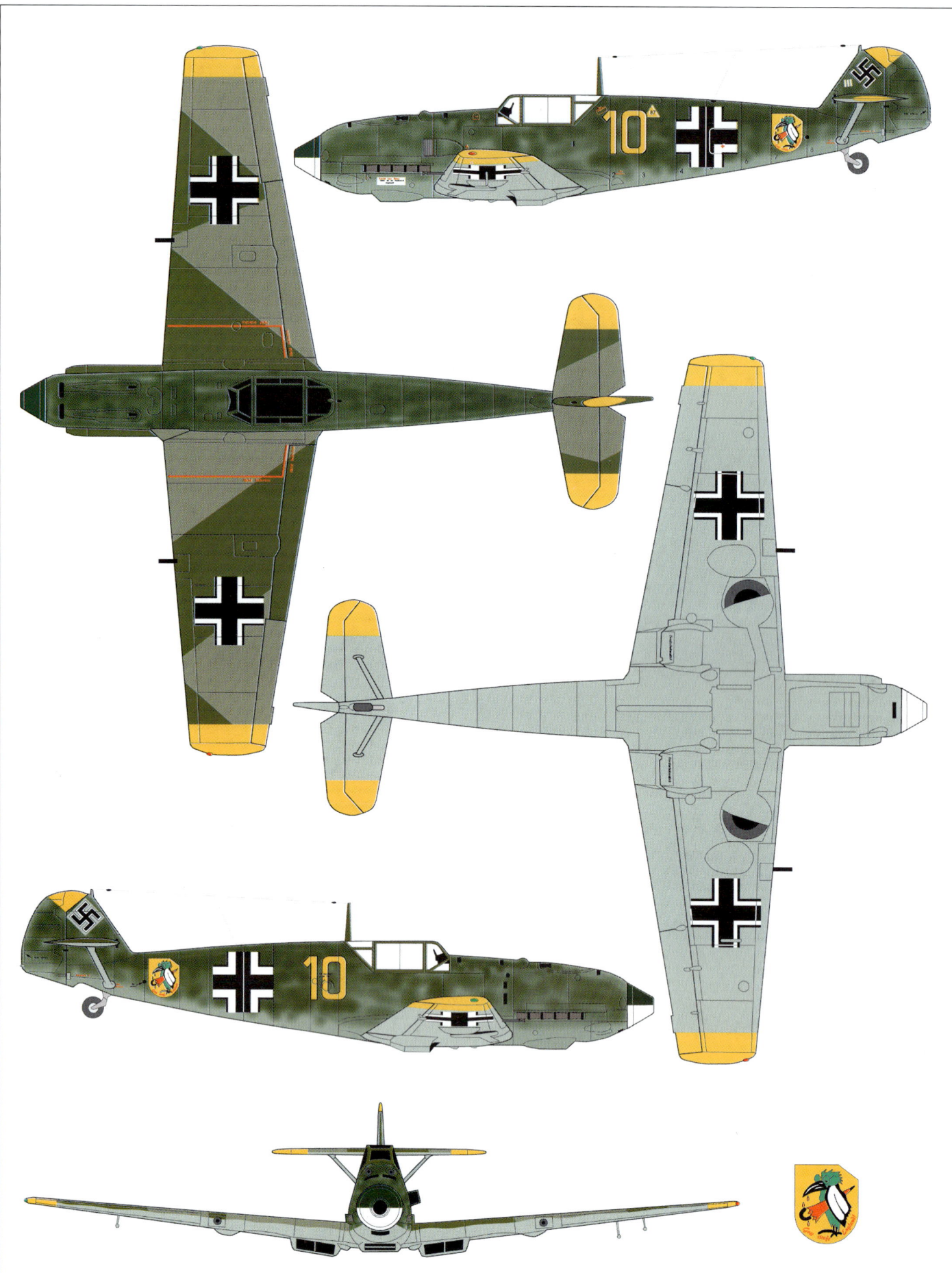

Messerschmitt Bf 109E-4 (W.Nr.5587) of 6./JG51, which crash-landed at East Langdon, Kent, on 24th August 1940, following an action above RAF Manston. Pilot Obfw. Fritz Beeck was taken prisoner. Although practically undamaged during the landing, this machine was rapidly stripped by souvenir hunters. The yellow areas were typical Luftwaffe recognition markings in mid August.

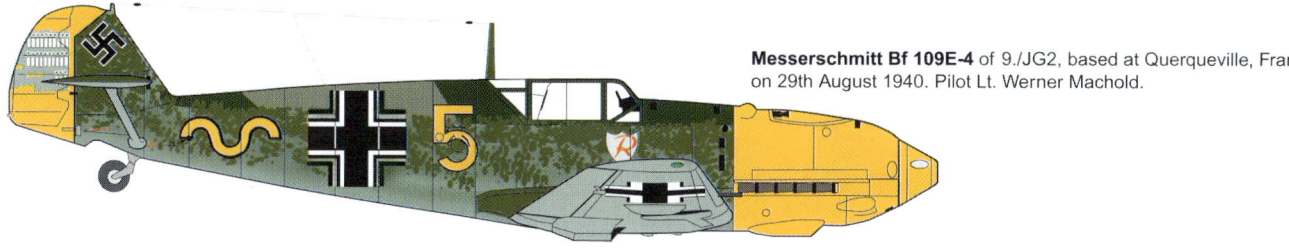

Messerschmitt Bf 109E-4 of 9./JG2, based at Querqueville, France, on 29th August 1940. Pilot Lt. Werner Machold.

Messerschmitt Bf 109E-4 of 9./JG2, based at Querqueville, France, on 29th August 1940. This was the aircraft immediately adjacent to the machine above and illustrates the diversity of style of markings to be found within the same unit and, in this case, on the same aircraft, where the numerals forming the 11 had been applied differently.

Messerschmitt Bf 109E-4 (W.Nr.5338) of 2./JG3, crash-landed near Pevensey Radar Station, Sussex, on 29th August 1940. Pilot Ofw. Bernard Lampskemper was captured.

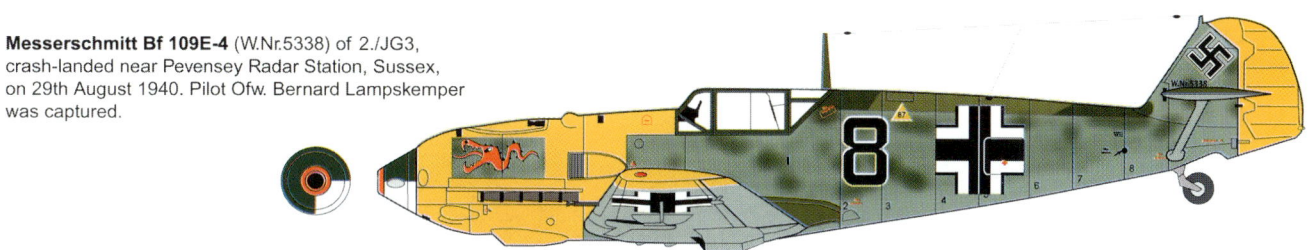

Messerschmitt Bf 109E-1 (W.Nr.3771) of 3./JG27, crash-landed at Westwood Court, Faversham, Kent, on 30th August 1940. Pilot Fw. Ernst Arnold (who was the wingman of Lt. Scherer, hence the scissor insignia) was captured.

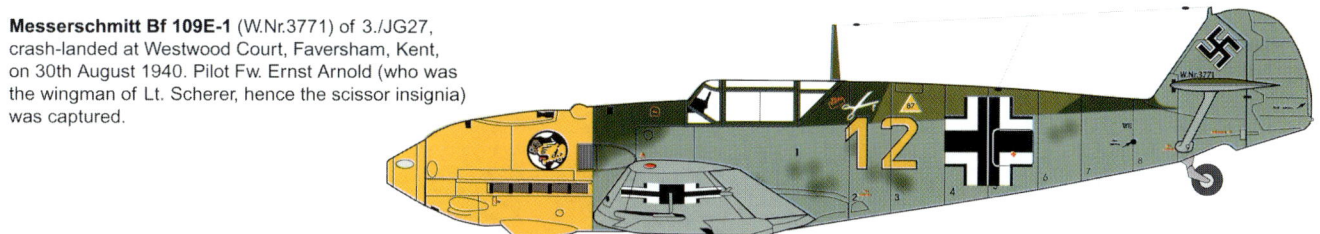

The RAF crash report stated: "12+ (yellow) Number 3271, engine cowling painted orange or yellow. Camouflage standard. (Fairly good condition)".

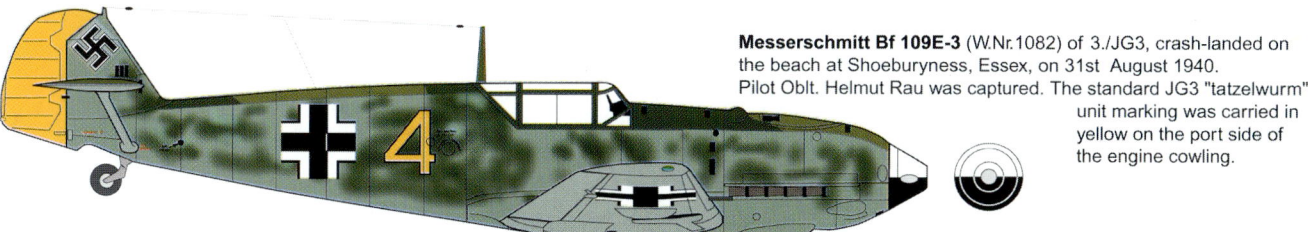

Messerschmitt Bf 109E-3 (W.Nr.1082) of 3./JG3, crash-landed on the beach at Shoeburyness, Essex, on 31st August 1940. Pilot Oblt. Helmut Rau was captured. The standard JG3 "tatzelwurm" unit marking was carried in yellow on the port side of the engine cowling.

The RAF crash report for this aircraft stated "+4 coloured yellow with black edges. Aircraft reported to be in good condition, but liable to be damaged owing to being partially covered at high water. Three stripes on tail, indicating three war flights". This aircraft was subsequently recovered for display, but the fabric surfaces had suffered considerably from immersion, as predicted.

Messerschmitt Bf 109E-4 (W.Nr.1184) of 9./JG26, crash-landed at Ulcombe, Kent, on 31st August 1940. Pilot Oblt. Wilhelm Fronhoefer was captured.

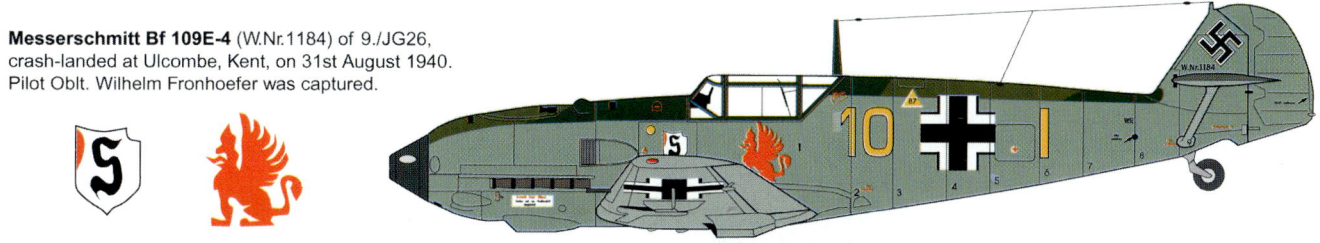

The RAF crash report for this aircraft stated "10+1 black Gothic S on white shield. No 62914. Pilot armour fitted. Camouflage green upper surfaces, light blue underneath".

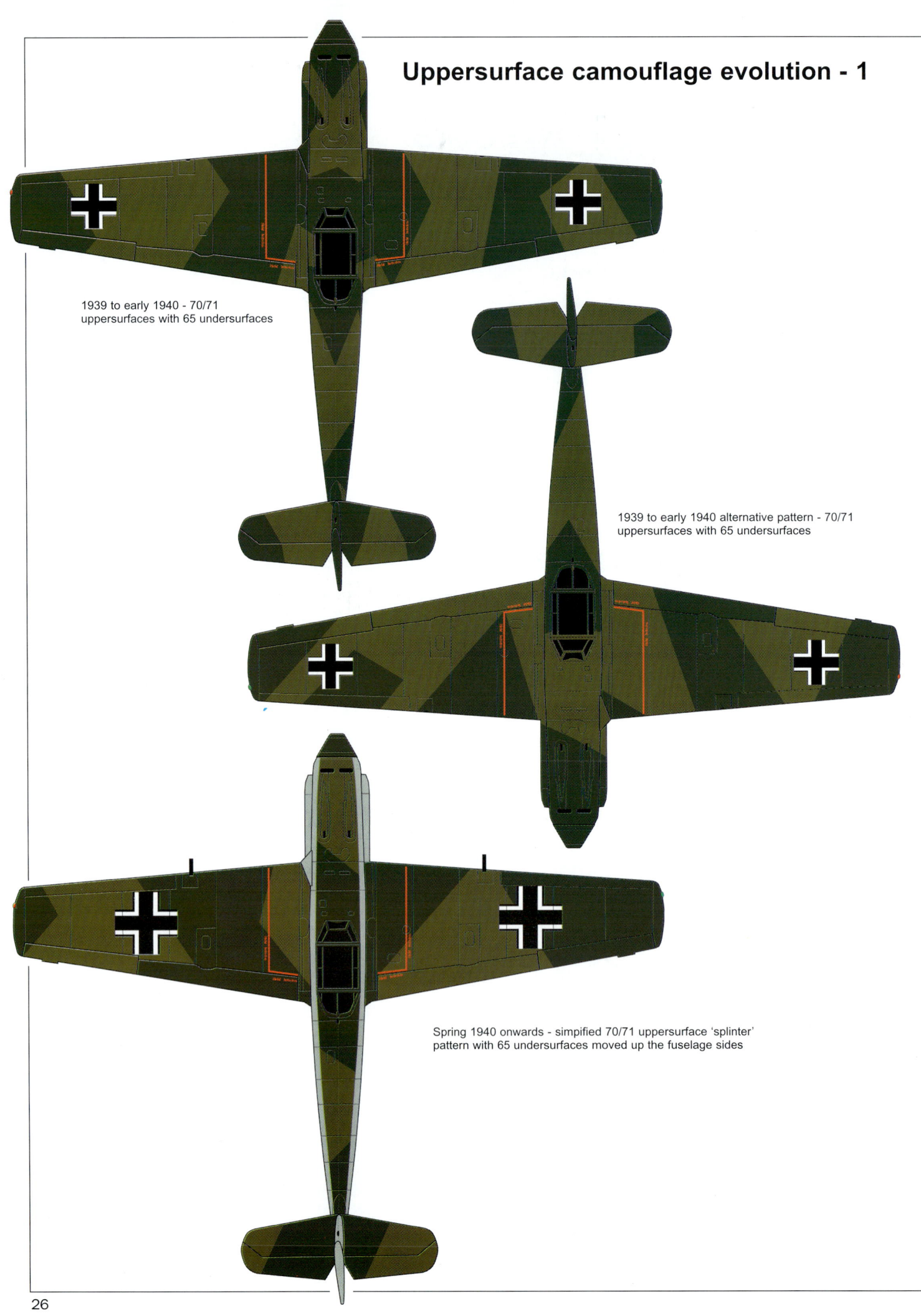

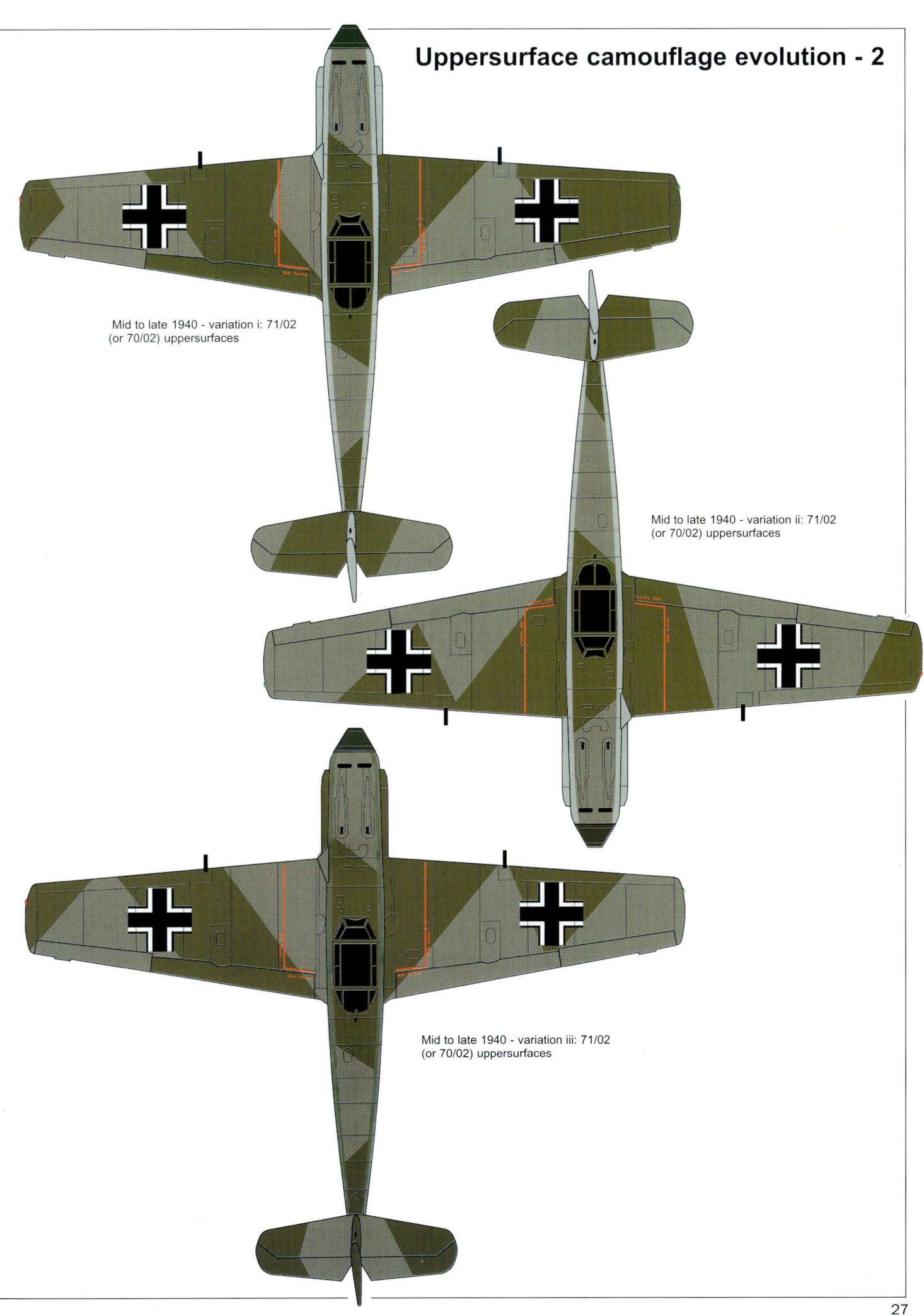

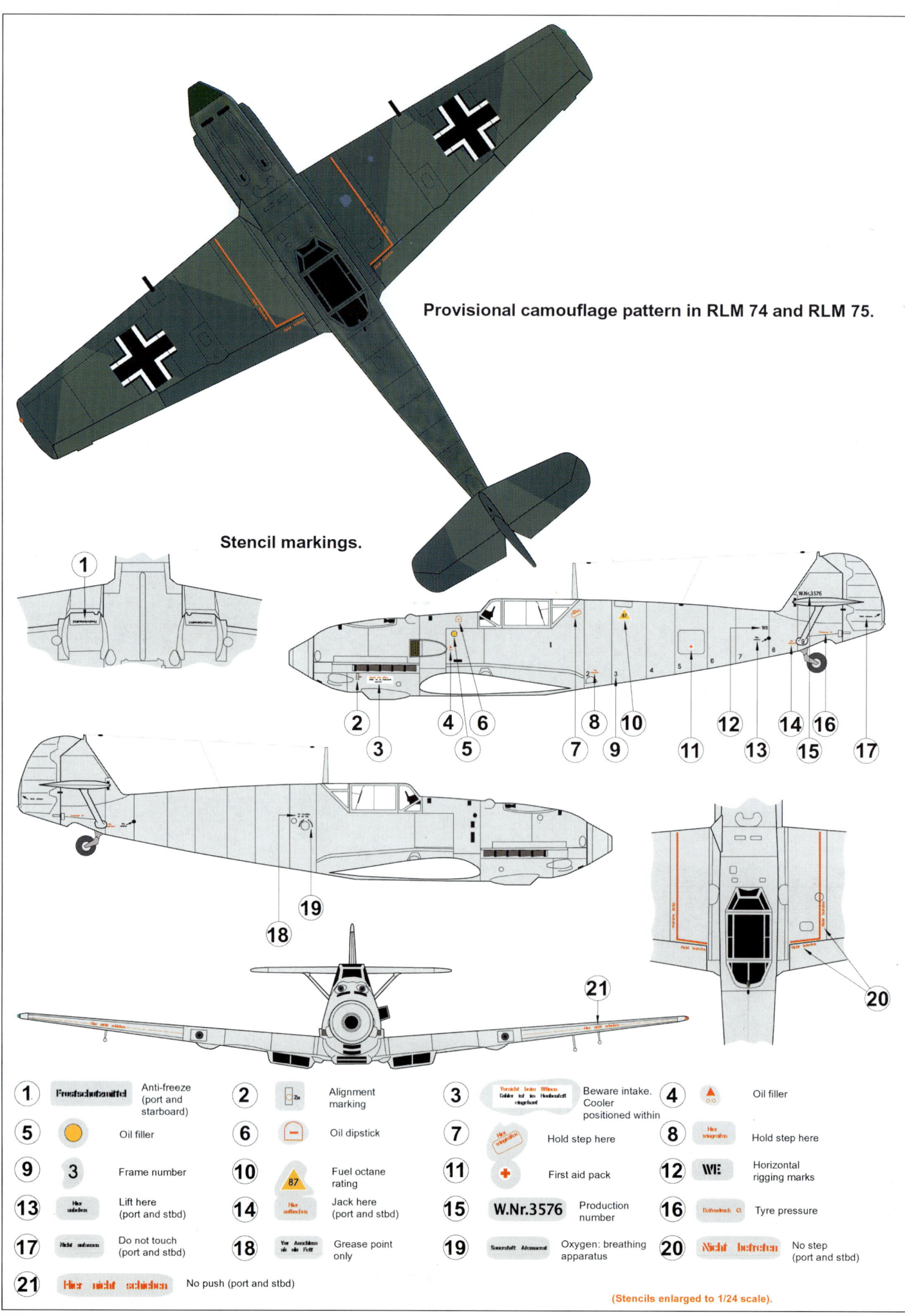

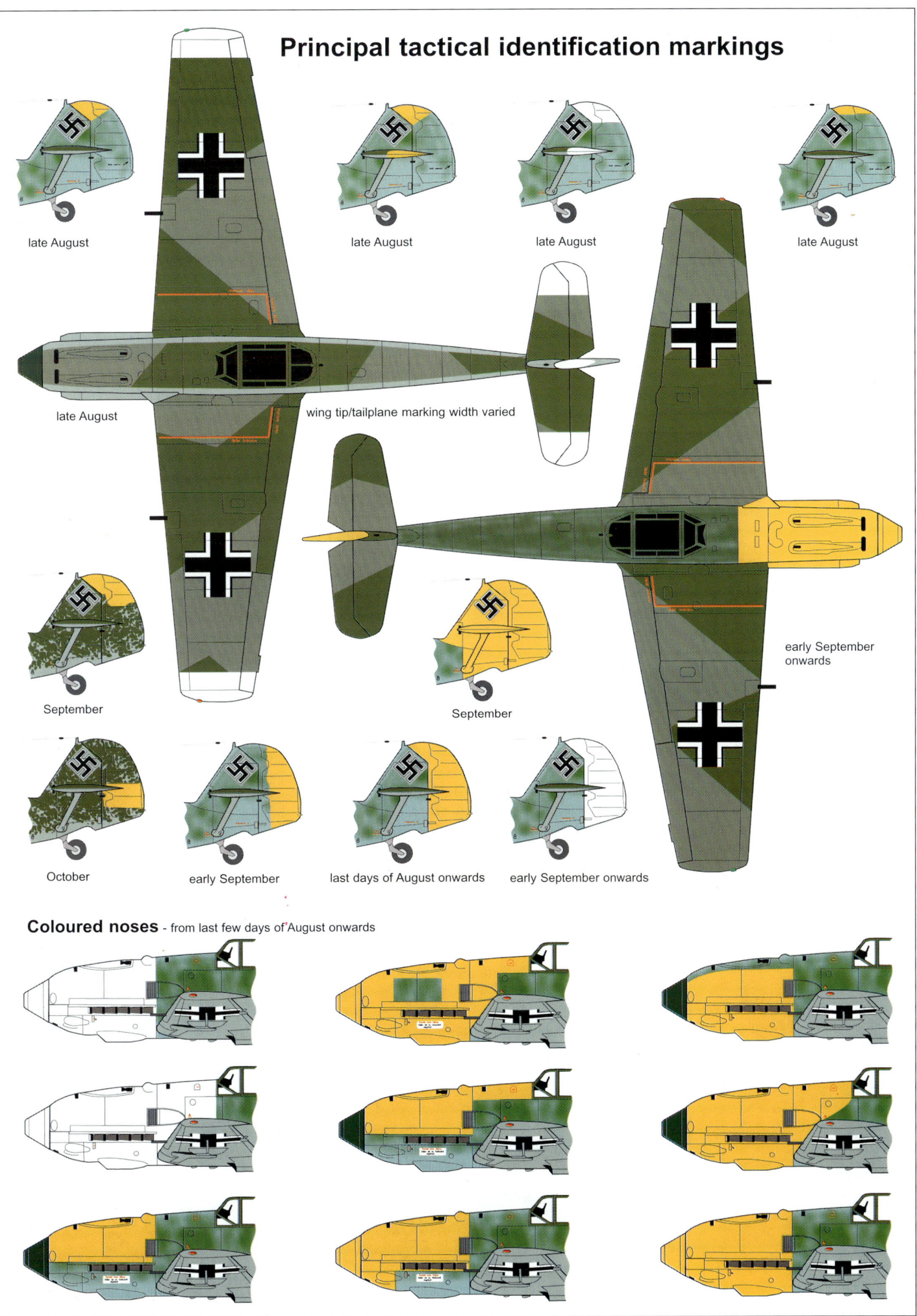

Messerschmitt Bf 109E-3/B of 2./LG2, crash-landed in France with operational damage on 31st August 1940.

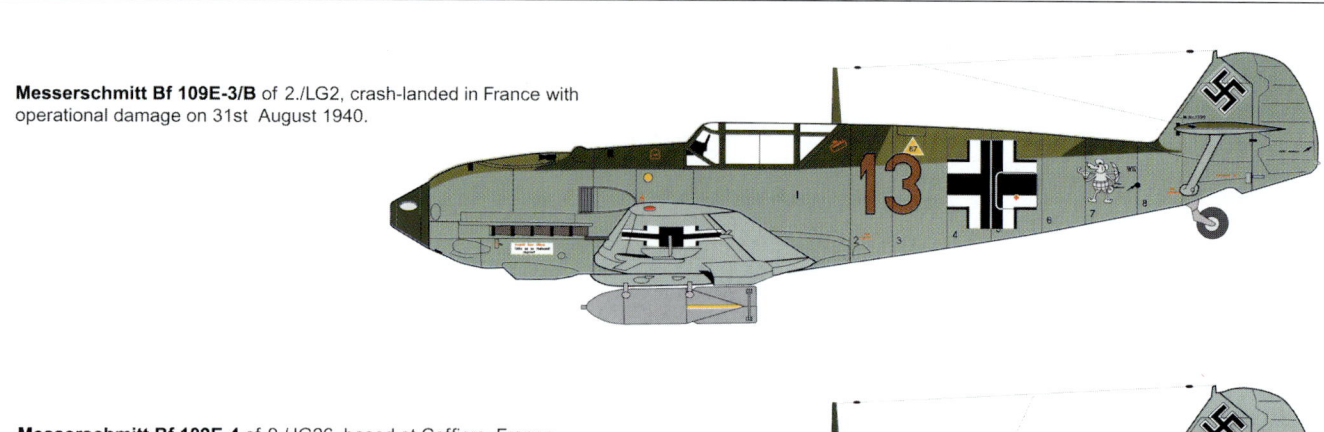

Messerschmitt Bf 109E-4 of 9./JG26, based at Caffiers, France, in August 1940.

Messerschmitt Bf 109E-4 of 3./JG2, based at Cherbourg-West, France, in September 1940.

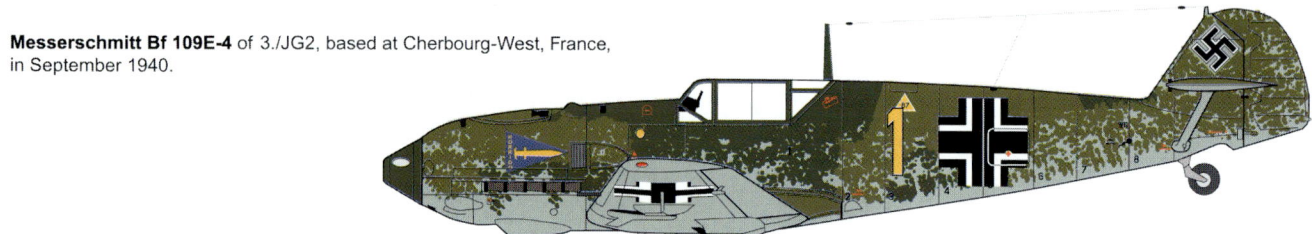

Messerschmitt Bf 109E-3 of 1./JG51, based at Pihen, France, in September 1940. Pilot Oblt. Heinz Bar.

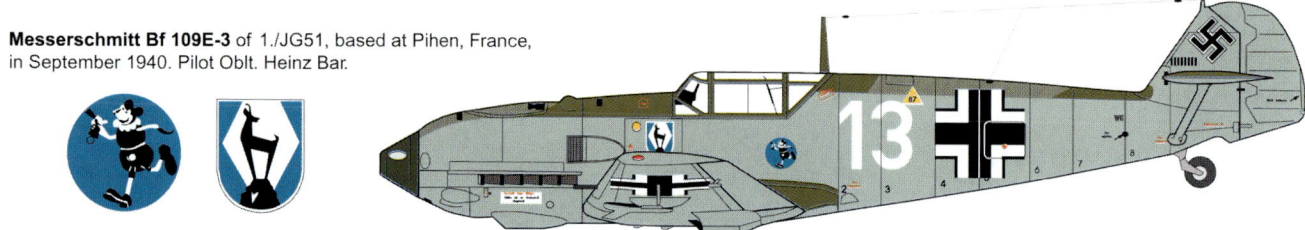

Messerschmitt Bf 109E-5 of 11./JG51, based at Wissant, France, in September 1940.

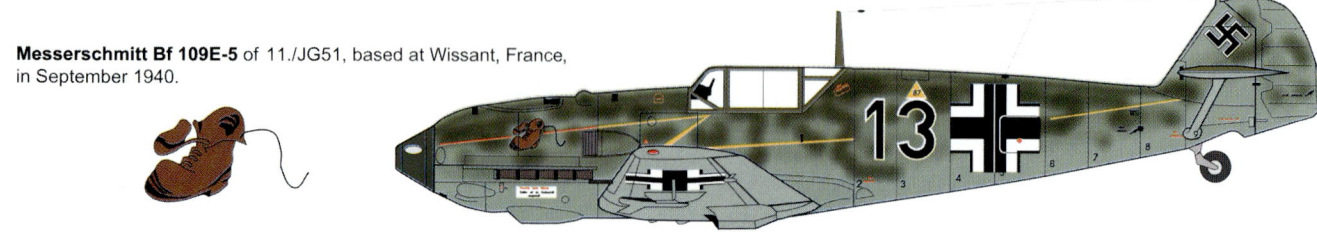

Messerschmitt Bf 109E-4 of 4./JG53. Based at Dinan, Channel Islands, in September 1940. Pilot Lt. Rudolf Lochner.

Messerschmitt Bf 109E-4 of Stab I./LG2, based at Calais-Marck, France, in September 1940.

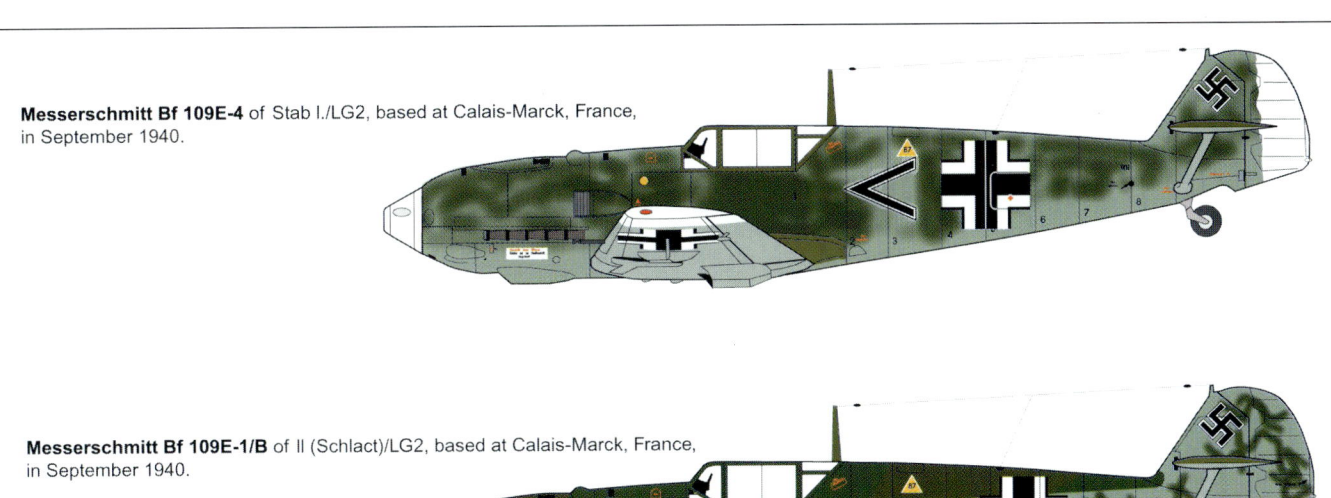

Messerschmitt Bf 109E-1/B of II (Schlact)/LG2, based at Calais-Marck, France, in September 1940.

Messerschmitt Bf 109E-1 of 2.(Jagd)/LG2, crash-landed at Calais-Marck, France, in September 1940.

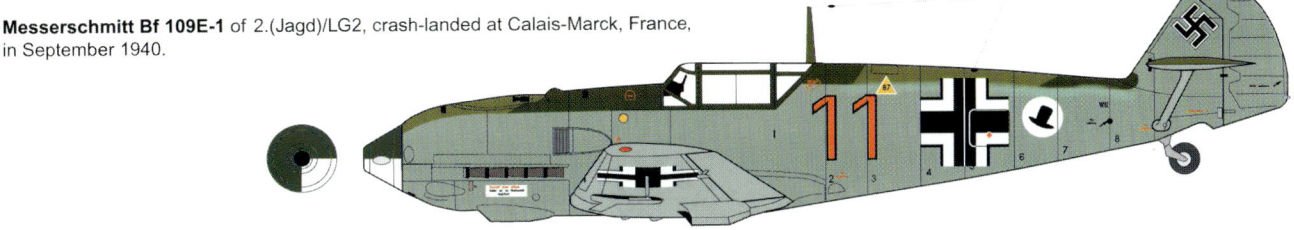

Messerschmitt Bf 109E-4 (W.Nr.1261) of 1./JG52, crash-landed at Sturry, Kent, on 2nd September 1940. Pilot Fw. Heinz Uhrlings was captured unhurt.

The RAF crash report for this aircraft stated "12+ (white) Wing tips and tail tips painted white. Aft half of rudder also painted white. Condition fair".

Messerschmitt Bf 109E-4 (W.Nr.3584) of 1./JG53, crash-landed at the Army firing ranges at Hythe, Kent, on 2nd September 1940. Pilot Uffz. Werner Karl was captured unhurt.

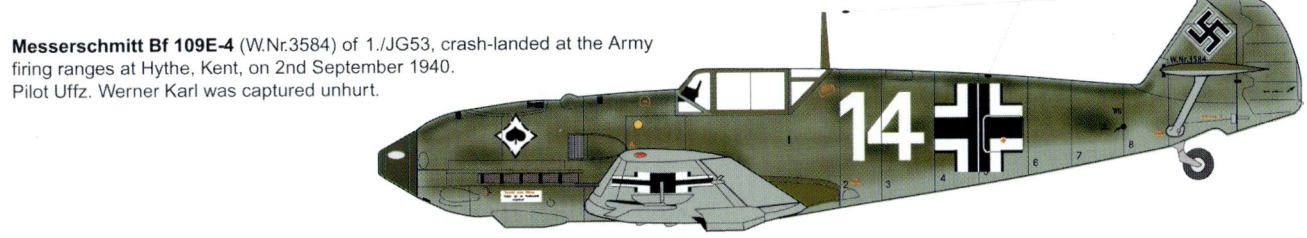

Messerschmitt Bf 109E-1 (W.Nr.3470) of 8./JG54, crash-landed at Kingsnorth, Kent, on 2nd September 1940. Pilot Fw. Heinrich Elbers was captured.

The RAF crash report for this aircraft stated "2+- (black) on fuselage just forward of windscreen. Camouflage top of fuselage dark green, sides of fuselage mottled light green, lower surfaces light blue. Wingtips and tail tip painted white. Spinner 3/4 white, one quarter black. Top of rudder painted white".

31

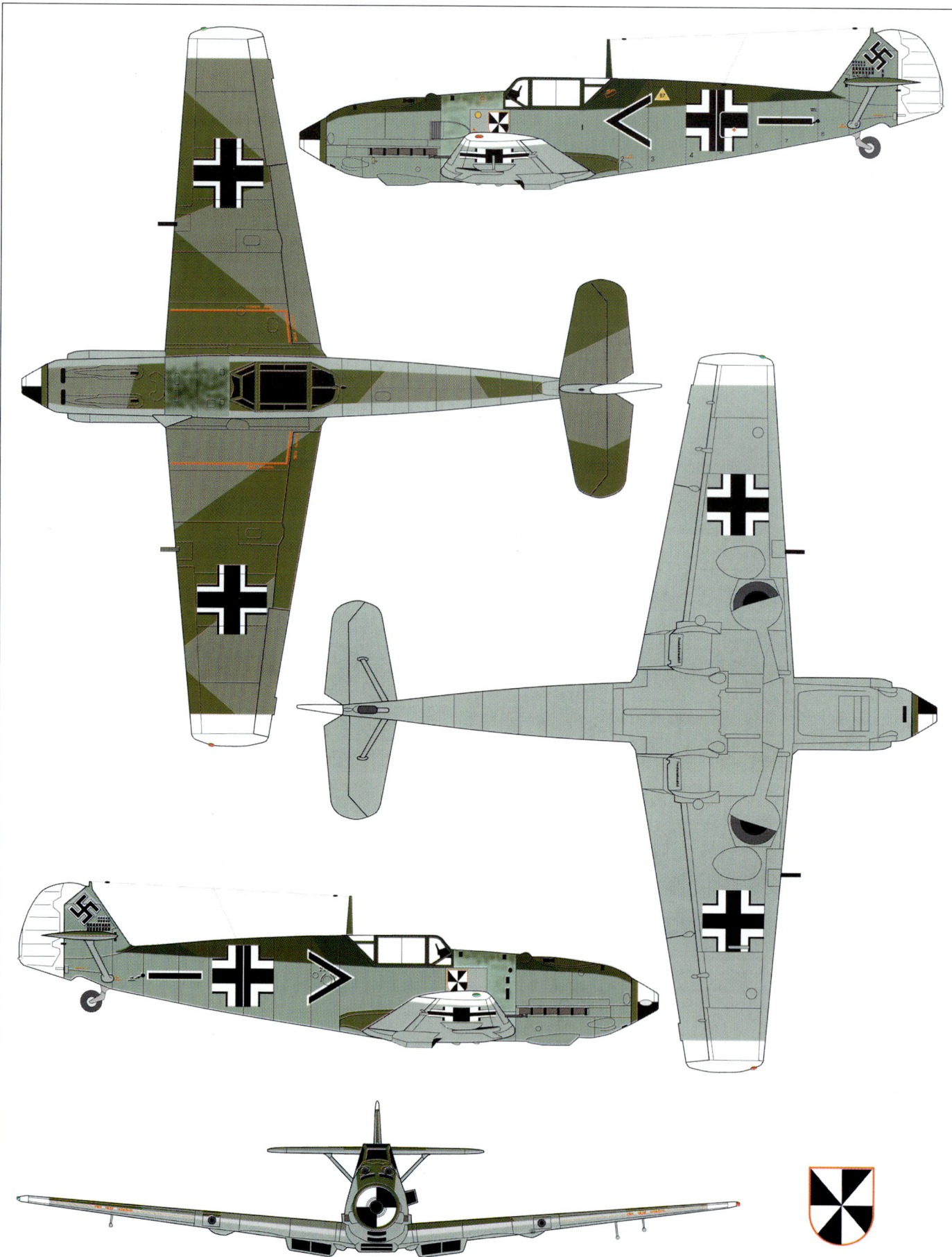

Messerschmitt Bf 109E-4 (W.Nr.1480) of Stab. II./JG3, which crash-landed at Love's Farm, Marden, Kent, on 5th September 1940, during the course of a diversionary sweep. It was shot down by F/Lt. J. T. Webster of 41 Squadron. Pilot Oblt. Franz von Werra (Gruppenadjutant) was captured, but subsequently escaped from a POW camp in Canada and returned to Germany. A replacement cowling section was fitted in place of the original and the wing leading edges were painted light grey in order to break up the head-on silhouette. The kill bars (abschussbalken) were arranged differently on either side of the tailfin. The RAF crash report stated "Markings -+< black outlined in white. Crest: shield U-shaped, outlined in red, divided into 8 segments coloured black and white. Wingtips and rudder painted white. Camouflage all blue. Fuselage all blue. Spinner divided into alternate black and white sectors. No armour".

Messerschmitt Bf 109E-4 (W.Nr.0750) of 3./JG3, crash-landed at Wichling, Kent, on 5th September 1940. Pilot Uffz. Heinz Grabow was captured unhurt. This aircraft was subsequently sent to Australia to promote recruitment within the RAAF.

The RAF crash report for this aircraft stated: "yellow 7, yellow tipped spinner followed by white and green segments. Crest white serpent, red tongue. White wingtips and rudder. No armour. Camouflage fuselage mottled dark and light green and grey. Wings standard".

Messerschmitt Bf 109E-4 (W.Nr.1985) of 1./JG3, crash-landed at Handen Farm, Aldington, Kent, on 5th September 1940. Pilot Lt. Heinz Schnabel was captured wounded.

The RAF crash report for this aircraft stated: "6+ (white outlined black) rudder white, wingtips white. Crest: white serpent (outlined in black) red tongue. 2 vertical stripes on rudder. Engine broken off".

Messerschmitt Bf 109E-1 of 2./JG3, crash-landed at Colombert, France, on 5th September 1940. Pilot Uffz. Keller.

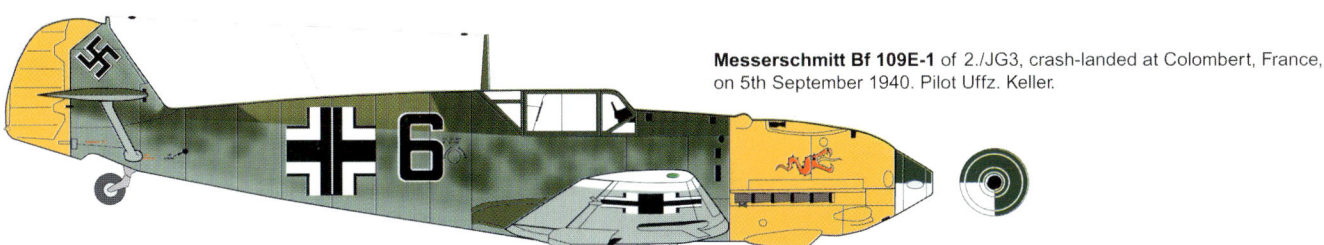

Messerschmitt Bf 109E-1 (W.Nr.5375) of Stab JG53, crash-landed at Monkton, Kent, on 5th September 1940. Pilot Hptm. Wilhelm Meyerweissflog was captured unhurt,

Two RAF crash reports were issued for this aircraft: ">1-+-- Cockpit armour. Camouflage light navy-grey, red band 1 foot broad round engine cowling. Red spinner and white wing tips. Rudder painted white" and "Markings -+-1> Camouflage mottled grey and blue with white wingtips. Vertical broad red band round cowling. Spinner half red, half white".

Messerschmitt Bf 109E-4 (W.Nr.2762) of 5./JG27, crashed at Tonbridge, Kent, on 6th September 1940. Pilot Fw. Erich Braun baled out safely and was taken prisoner.

Messerschmitt Bf 109E-1 of 7./JG27, crash-landed at Blean, Kent, on 6th September 1940. Pilot Uffz. Ernst Nittmann was captured unhurt.

The RAF crash report for this aircraft stated: "Engine cowling white. White 8 on grey rectangular background. Shield with St. Peter's cross with 3 Me.109 in power dive in gold".

Messerschmitt Bf 109E-4 (W.Nr.1506) of 7./JG53, crash-landed on Vincent's Farm, outside RAF Manston, Kent, on 6th September 1940. Pilot Uffz. Hans-Georg Schulte was taken prisoner. The swastika had been overpainted as a unit protest against Goering's order to overpaint the unit marking which had, in turn, been overpainted by the white nose.

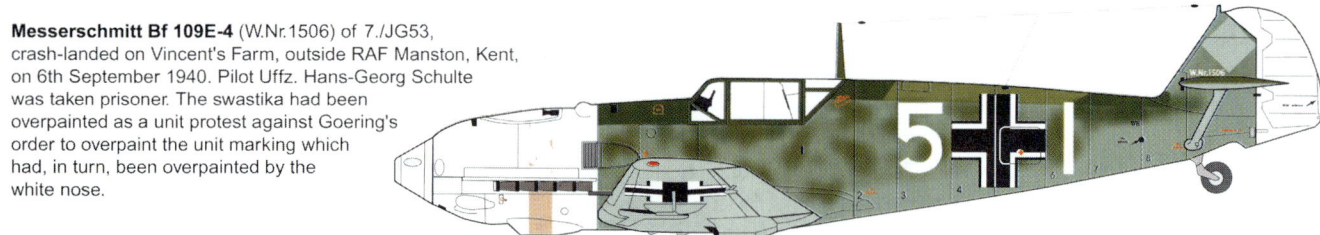

The RAF crash report for this aircraft stated: "5+1 (white) white cowling, spinner and rudder. Camouflage mottled light and dark green and grey. Thick red band round cowling painted out. Number 1506. Condition fair. Pilot armour".

Messerschmitt Bf 109E-4/B (W.Nr. 5567) of 6./II (Schlacht) LG2, crash-landed at RAF Hawkinge, Kent, on 6th September 1940. Pilot Fw. Werner Gottschalk was captured unhurt.

The RAF crash report for this aircraft stated: "+C black triangle outlined white, yellow C. White rudder, wingtips, white having been painted on yellow spinner, blue and white vertical stripes. Plate BF109E-4/B number 5567. Camouflage two shades of grey on upper surfaces, standard duck egg blue lower surfaces".

Messerschmitt Bf 109E-4 of 1./JG77, crash-landed at Rolvenden, Kent, on 7th September 1940. Pilot Ofw. Gotthard Goltzsche was taken prisoner. Sections of wing panelling now held by the Battle of Britain Museum at Hawkinge are in RLM 70 and RLM 02.

The RAF crash report for this aircraft stated: "11+ yellow cowling, rudder, spinner. Camouflage grey speckled on top. Good condition".

Messerschmitt Bf 109E-1/B (W.Nr.6316) of 7./JG3, crash-landed at Flimwell, Kent, on 9th September 1940. Pilot Uffz. Matthias Massmann was captured unhurt. It was not possible to determine the spinner paint scheme from the photo on which this profile is based, but one source stated it to be as shown.

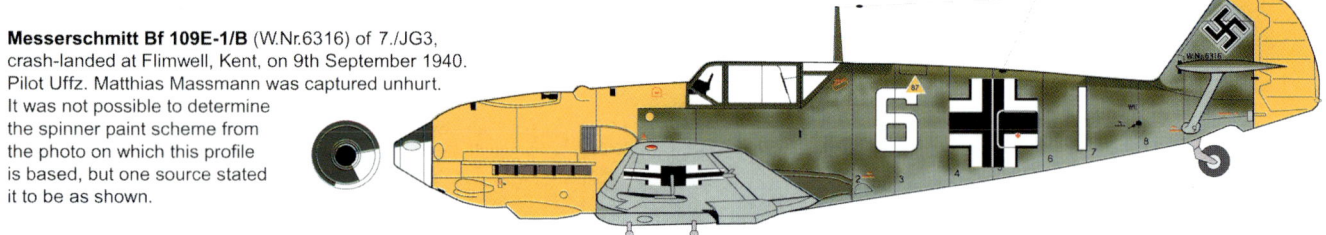

The RAF crash report for this aircraft stated: "-6+1 yellow spinner and rudder. Good condition. Bomb rack. Pilot armour".

Messerschmitt Bf 109E-4 (W.Nr.1394) of Stab I./JG27, crash-landed at Mayfield, Sussex, on 9th. September 1940. Pilot Oblt. Gunther Bode (Gruppe Adjutant) was captured unhurt.

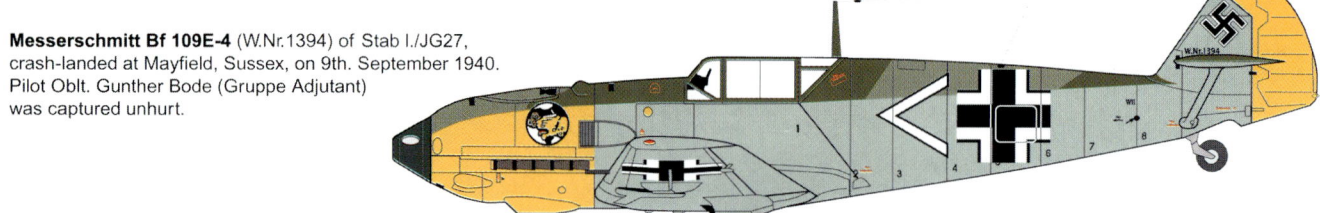

The RAF crash report for this aircraft stated: "<+ yellow nose and rudder. Crest on nose, yellow jaguar's head with smiling negress wearing white earring. Number 1394. No bomb rack, no armour".

Messerschmitt Bf 109E-1/B (W.Nr.3488) of 5./JG27. Crash-landed at Storrington, Sussex, on 9th. September 1940. Plot Oblt. Erwin Daig was captured unhurt.

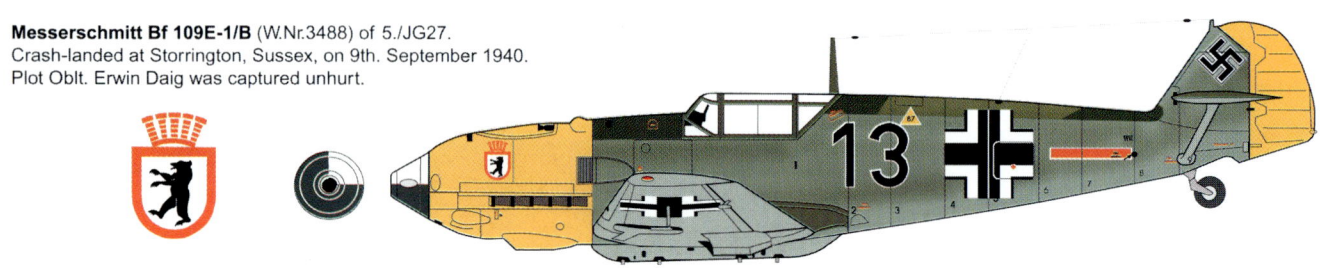

The RAF crash report for this aircraft stated: "13+- (long red dash with white edging) Cowling and rudder yellow. ETC50 bomb rack".

Messerschmitt Bf 109E-1/B (W.Nr.6147) of 2./JG27,
crash-landed at Isfield, Sussex, on 15th. September 1940.
Pilot Uffz. Andreas Wallburger was captured unhurt.

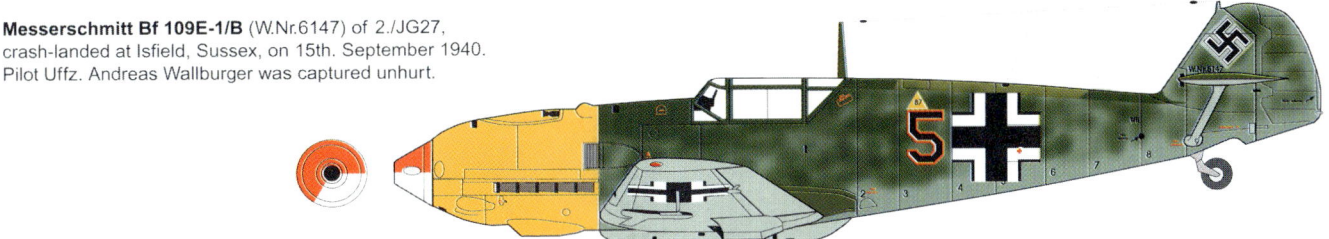

The RAF crash report for this aircraft stated: "5+ all yellow nose. Spinner red and white. Old markings rubbed out BZ+NG Number 6147 Large bomb rack fitted".

Messerschmitt Bf 109E-4/B of 3./LG2, crash-landed at Shellness,
Isle of Sheppey, Kent, on 15th. September 1940.
Pilot Uffz. August Klick was captured unhurt.

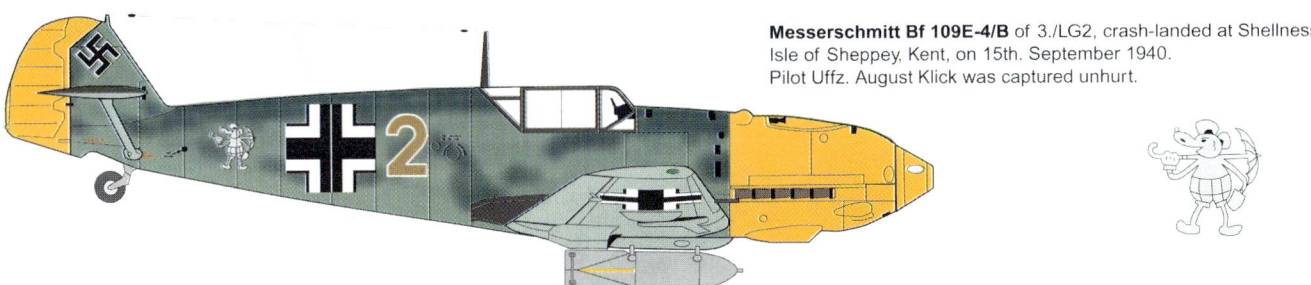

The RAF crash report for this aircraft stated: "2+ (brown with white edge). Yellow nose cowling, spinner and rudder. Camouflage cloudy grey on fuselage, battleship grey uppersurfaces and light blue lower surfaces".

Messerschmitt Bf 109E-1 (W.Nr.6294) of 7./JG26,
crash-landed at Camber, Sussex, on 17th September 1940.
Pilot Uffz. Karl-Heinz Bock was captured unhurt.

The RAF crash report for this aircraft stated: "Markings I+2 (coloured white, outlined in black). Yellow nose. Number 6294. No head shield.
Aircraft generally appears standard".

Messerschmitt Bf 109E-1 (W.Nr.2674) of 9./JG27,
crash-landed at Royal St. George's Golf Course,
Sandwich, Kent, on 18th September 1940.
Pilot Gef. W. Gloeckner was captured.

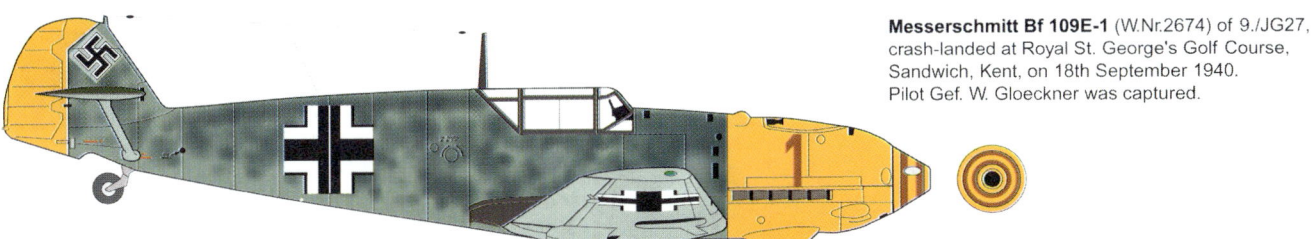

The RAF crash report for this aircraft stated: "Yellow nose with figure 1 on cowling (not on fuselage). Three concentric brown rings on spinner.
Aircraft set on fire by pilot after good belly landing".

Messerschmitt Bf 109E-1/B (W.Nr.6321) of 9./JG27, crash-landed at Sellindge, Kent,
on 18th September 1940. Pilot Fw. Ernst Schultz was captured,
but died later from his injuries.

The RAF crash report for this aircraft stated: "Markings yellow nose with large 7 in brown on cowling (not on fuselage).
Three concentric brown rings on spinner. Yellow rudder. Bomb rack".

Messerschmitt Bf 109E-4 of 1./JG2, based at Beaumont-le-Roger,
France, in September 1940. The remains of the underwing
Stammkennzeichen were still present.

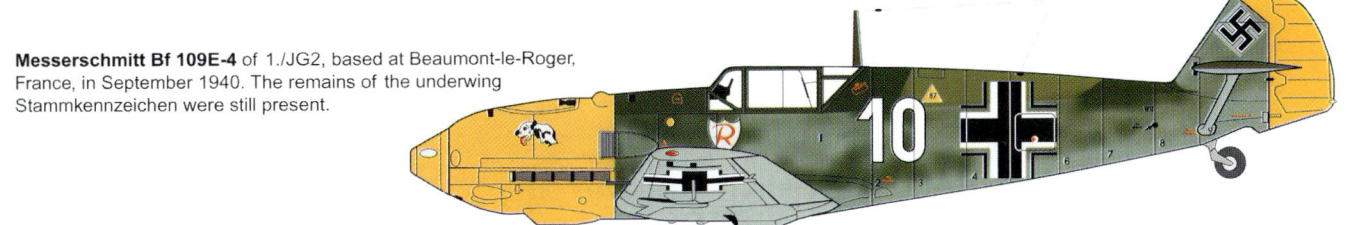

Messerschmitt Bf 109E-4 of 3./JG2, based at Cherbourg-West, France, in September 1940.

Messerschmitt Bf 109E-4 of 7./JG2, based at Le Havre, France, in September 1940. Pilot Oblt. Werner Machold.

Messerschmitt Bf 109E-4 of 7./JG2, based at Beaumont-le-Roger, France, in September 1940.

Messerschmitt Bf 109E-4 of 9./JG2, based at Le Havre, France, in September 1940.

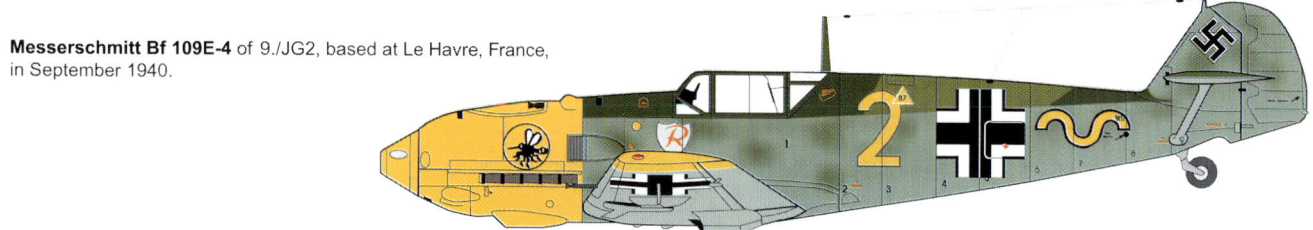

Messerschmitt Bf 109E-4 of I./JG3, based at Grandvillers, France, in September 1940. Pilot Hptm. Hans von Hahn.

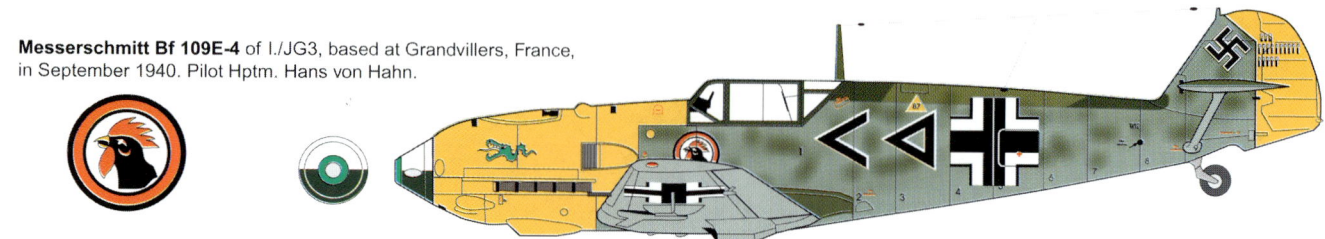

Messerschmitt Bf 109E-4 of 1./JG3, based at Grandvillers, France, in September 1940.

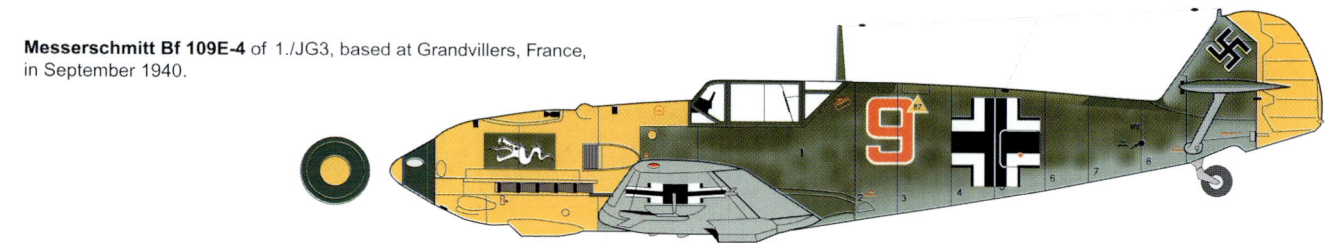

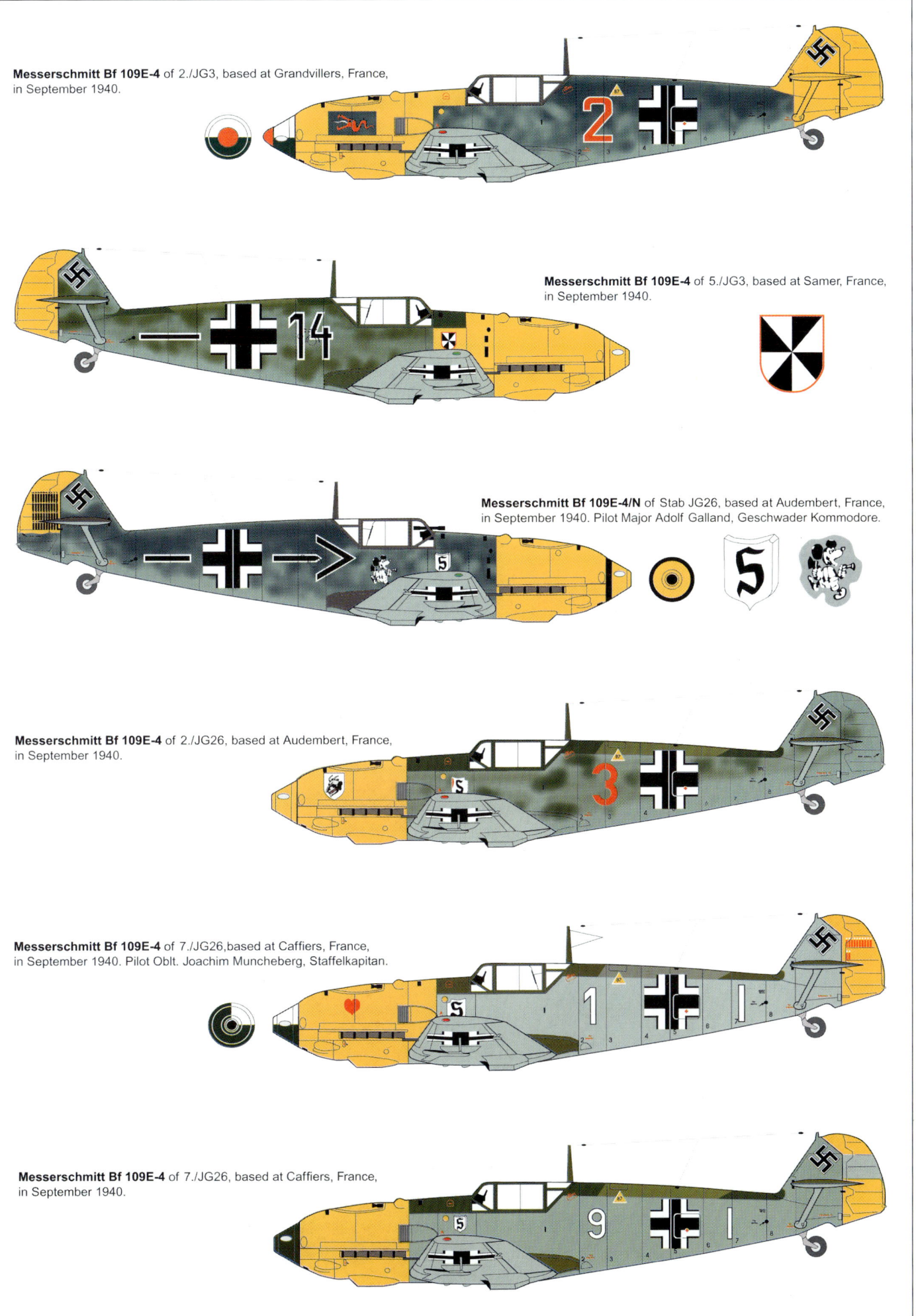

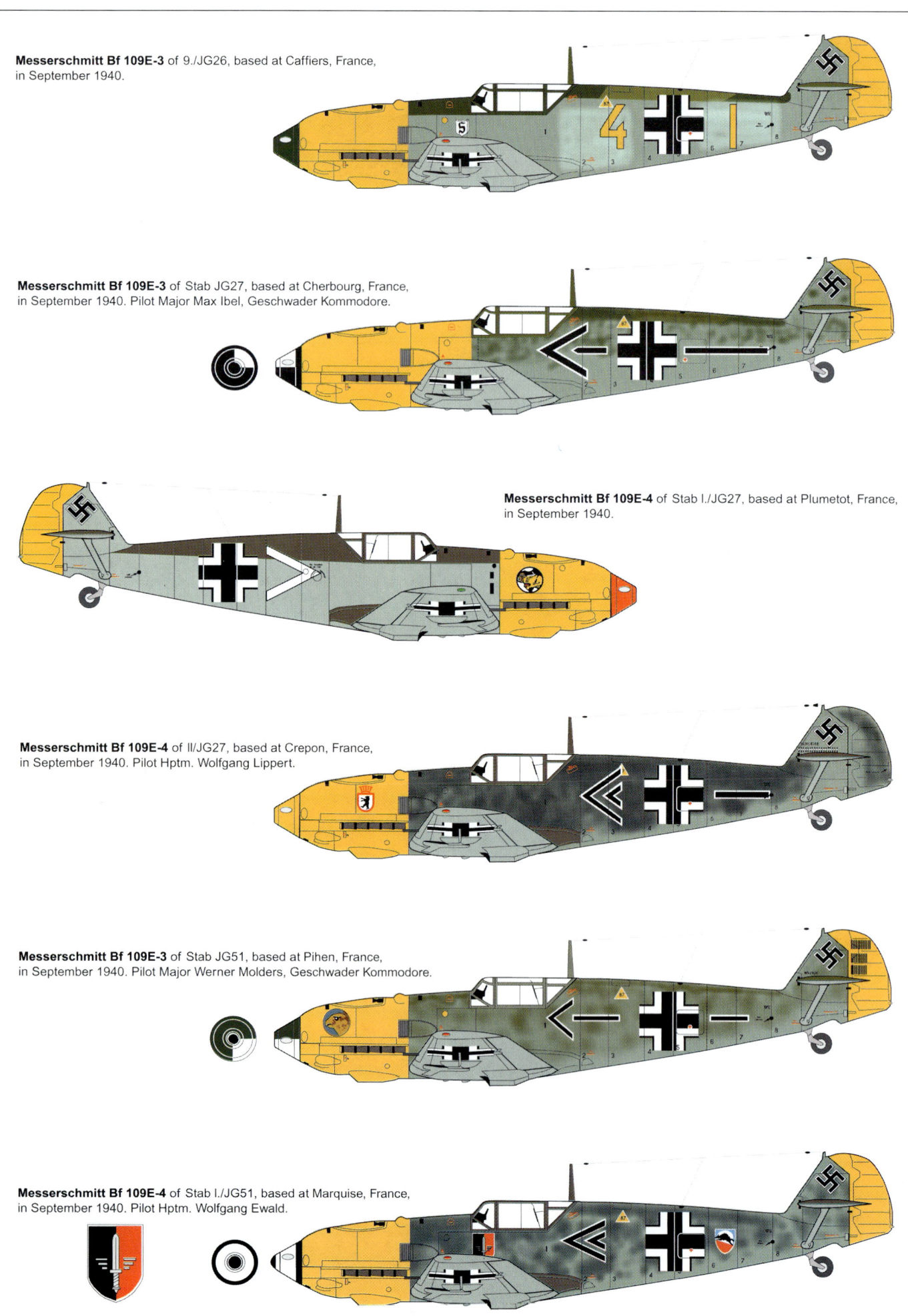

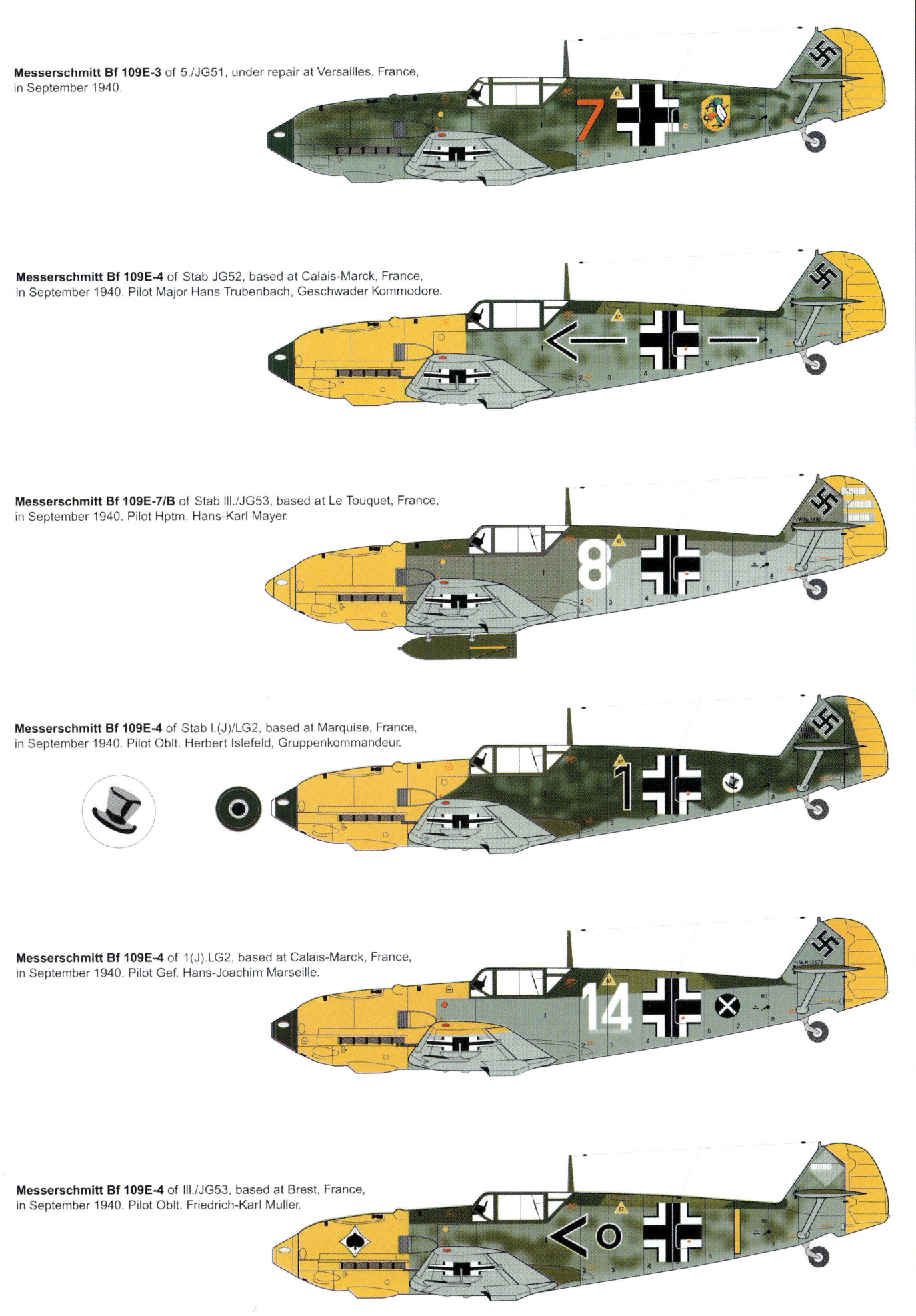

Messerschmitt Bf 109E-3 of 5./JG51, under repair at Versailles, France, in September 1940.

Messerschmitt Bf 109E-4 of Stab JG52, based at Calais-Marck, France, in September 1940. Pilot Major Hans Trubenbach, Geschwader Kommodore.

Messerschmitt Bf 109E-7/B of Stab III./JG53, based at Le Touquet, France, in September 1940. Pilot Hptm. Hans-Karl Mayer.

Messerschmitt Bf 109E-4 of Stab I.(J)/LG2, based at Marquise, France, in September 1940. Pilot Oblt. Herbert Isleifeld, Gruppenkommandeur.

Messerschmitt Bf 109E-4 of 1(J).LG2, based at Calais-Marck, France, in September 1940. Pilot Gef. Hans-Joachim Marseille.

Messerschmitt Bf 109E-4 of III./JG53, based at Brest, France, in September 1940. Pilot Oblt. Friedrich-Karl Muller.

39

Messerschmitt Bf 109E-4 (W.Nr.1190) of 4./JG26, crash-landed at Eastdene, Sussex, on 30th. September 1940. Pilot Uffz. Horst Perez was captured unhurt. This machine was exhibited in the USA and has subsequently been restored and put on display at the Imperial War Museum, Duxford. Several large pieces of original wing structure are on display at the Battle of Britain Museum at Hawkinge.

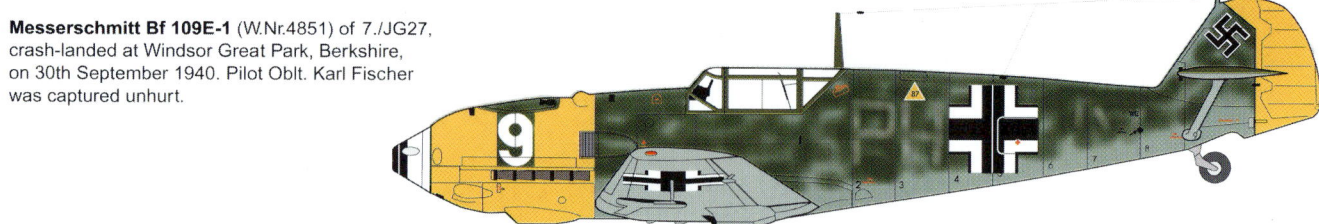

The RAF crash report for this aircraft stated: "Markings 4+- Marking had previously been <+ Crest: tiger's head in natural colours on port side of fuselage. White shield with black F in addition. Yellow nose and fin. Number 1190. 100 octane marking in triangle marked on fuselage".

Messerschmitt Bf 109E-1 (W.Nr.4851) of 7./JG27, crash-landed at Windsor Great Park, Berkshire, on 30th September 1940. Pilot Oblt. Karl Fischer was captured unhurt.

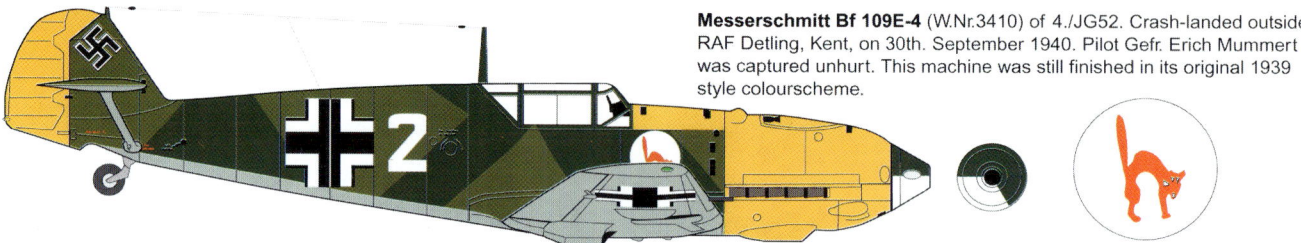

The RAF crash report for this aircraft stated: "9 painted on yellow cowling. Spinner white with black circle on tip. Old markings had been painted over viz. PH+LV Pilot armour".

Messerschmitt Bf 109E-4 (W.Nr.3410) of 4./JG52. Crash-landed outside RAF Detling, Kent, on 30th. September 1940. Pilot Gefr. Erich Mummert was captured unhurt. This machine was still finished in its original 1939 style colourscheme.

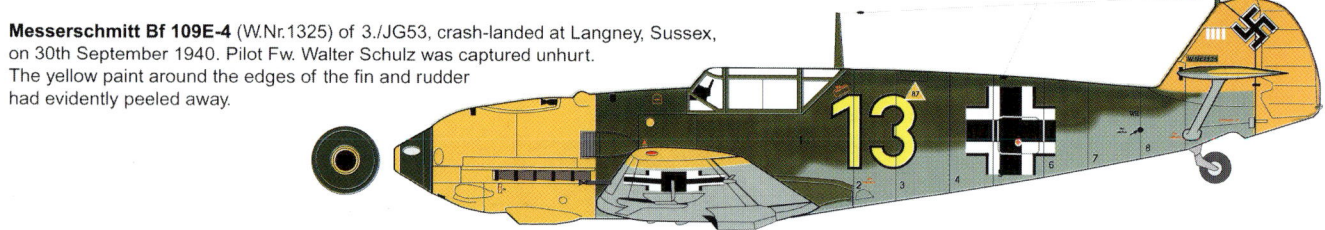

The RAF crash report for this aircraft stated: "Markings 2+ (2 in white). The markings had previously been 8+ but this was painted out. Yellow nose and rudder. Green spinner with one sector white. Circular shield".

Messerschmitt Bf 109E-4 (W.Nr.1325) of 3./JG53, crash-landed at Langney, Sussex, on 30th September 1940. Pilot Fw. Walter Schulz was captured unhurt. The yellow paint around the edges of the fin and rudder had evidently peeled away.

The RAF crash report for this aircraft stated: "13+ (figures in yellow). Orange nose, rudder and fin".

Messerschmitt Bf 109E-1 (W.Nr.5175) of 7./JG53. Crash-landed at Strood, Kent, on 30th. September 1940. Pilot Uffz. Ernst Poschenrieder was captured badly wounded. The wing leading edges were painted light grey to break up the end-on silhouette.

The RAF crash report for this aircraft stated: "12+I (all in white). Yellow nose and rudder. Pilot head armour. Camouflage blue and green dappled yellow and green on upper surface, sky blue beneath".

Messerschmitt Bf 109E-4/B (W.Nr.5814) of 1./JG51, crashed at Shadoxhurst, Kent, on 1st October 1940. Pilot Uffz. Edward Garnith baled out and was captured.

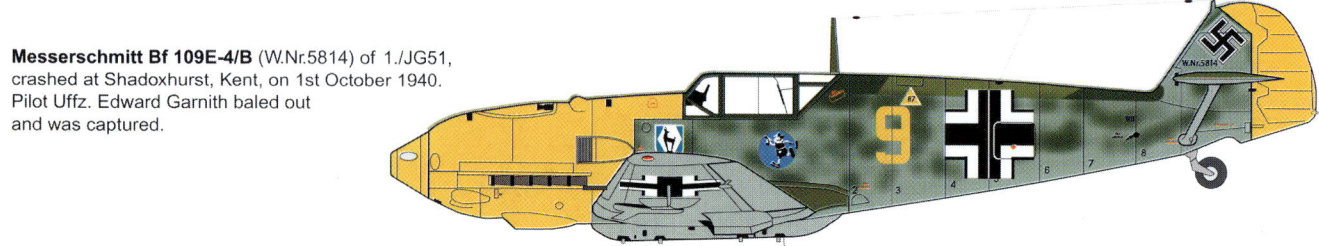

The RAF crash report for this aircraft stated: "Yellow 9+ and yellow nose and rudder. Bomb rack".

Messerschmitt Bf 109E-4/B (W.Nr.5801) of 8./JG53, crash-landed at Addelstead Farm, East Peckham, London, on 2nd October 1940. Pilot Lt. Walter Fiel was captured unhurt.

The RAF crash report for this aircraft stated: "7+I black letters outlined in white. Yellow nose with red band, red spinner. Head armour. Centre-line bomb rack".

Messerschmitt Bf 109E-4 (W.Nr.1804) of 1./JG53, crash-landed at Aldington, Kent, on 5th October 1940. Pilot Uffz. Wilhelm Gehsla was captured wounded.

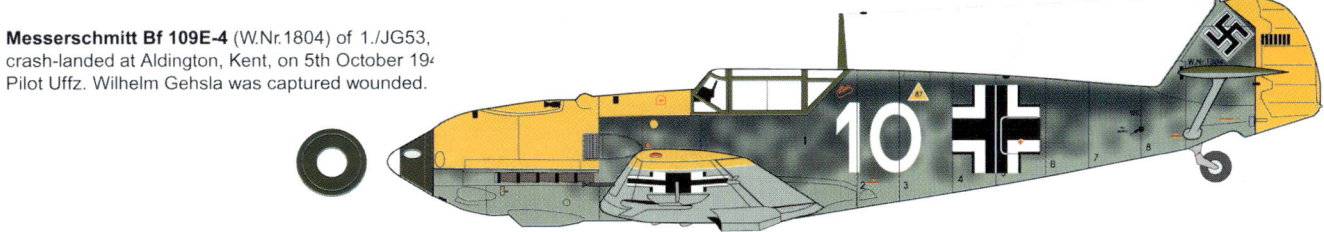

The RAF crash report for this aircraft stated: "10+ white. Nose and rudder yellow. Number 1804. Camouflage grey, dappled black, carefully done".

Messerschmitt Bf 109E-4/B (W.Nr.3726) of 6./LG2, crash-landed at Peasmarsh, Sussex, on 5th October 1940. Pilot Fw. Erhardt Pankrantz was captured wounded.

The RAF crash report for this aircraft stated: "Markings M+△ I   M in yellow △ and I in black. Nose and rudder yellow. Spinner pale blue with white tip. Crest: black cat in spurred boots holding a lantern. All in a black circle. Number 1723. Pilot head armour".

Messerschmitt Bf 109E-4/B (W.Nr.4103) of 2./JG51, crash-landed at Guestling, Sussex, on 7th October 1940. Pilot Oblt. Victor Molders, Staffelkapitan (and brother of Werner Molders) was captured.

The RAF crash report for this aircraft stated: "Nose and rudder yellow. Large bomb rack fitted".

Messerschmitt Bf 109E-4/B (W.Nr.5566) of 4.(S)/LG2, crashed onto the Tunbridge Wells Golf Course, Kent, on 7th October 1940. Pilot Uffz. G. Morschell was captured wounded.

The RAF crash report for this aircraft stated: " +F Burnt out. Triangle is black outlined in white. An old marking was visible KB+IF. Nose and rudder yellow. No head armour. Large bomb rack fitted".

Messerschmitt Bf 109E-1 (W.Nr.3465) of 4./JG52. Crash-landed at Little Grange Farm, Woodham Mortimer, Essex, on 8th. October 1940. Pilot Fw. Paul Boche was captured wounded.

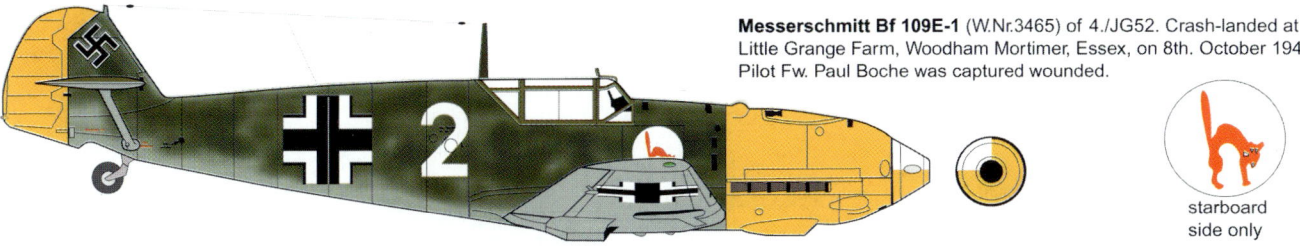

starboard side only

The RAF crash report for this aircraft stated: "2+ (white) Crest: red cat in large white circle. Yellow nose and rudder. Spinner yellow with white segment. Number 3465. Driving mirror fixed to enable pilot to see to the rear".

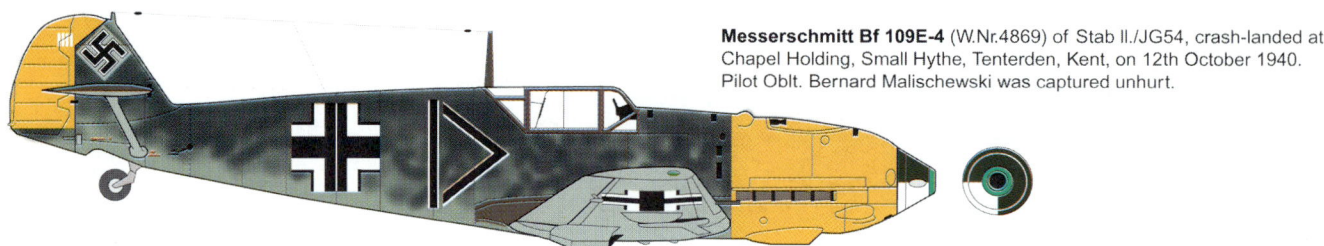

Messerschmitt Bf 109E-4 (W.Nr.4869) of Stab II./JG54, crash-landed at Chapel Holding, Small Hythe, Tenterden, Kent, on 12th October 1940. Pilot Oblt. Bernard Malischewski was captured unhurt.

The RAF crash report for this aircraft stated: "Markings <I+ the horizontal vee and vertical bar consist of alternate black and white stripes of different thicknesses".

Messerschmitt Bf 109E-4/B (W.Nr.0860) of 7./JG3, crash-landed at Cuckold Coombe, Wye, Kent, on 13th. October 1940. Pilot Gef. Hubert Rungen was captured.

The RAF crash report for this aircraft stated: "7+I the figures I and 7 are white with black edging. Number 860. Bomb rack fitted'.

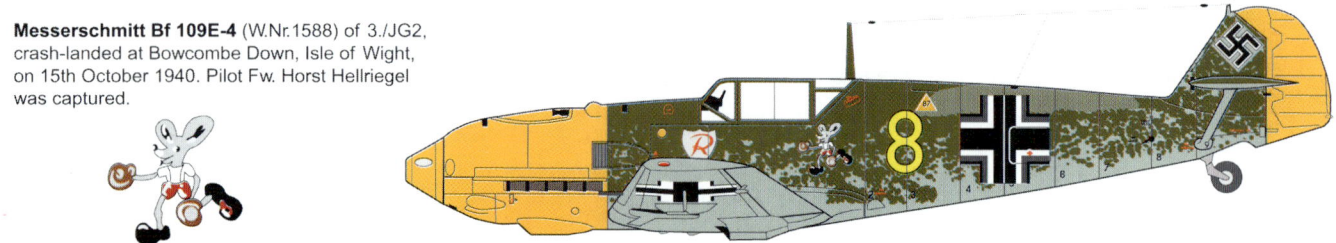

Messerschmitt Bf 109E-4 (W.Nr.1588) of 3./JG2, crash-landed at Bowcombe Down, Isle of Wight, on 15th October 1940. Pilot Fw. Horst Hellriegel was captured.

The RAF crash report for this aircraft stated: "8+ (8 is yellow outlined black). Cowling and rudder orange yellow. Crest: a red "R" in script on a silver shield with red outline. On opposite side of fuselage, a "Mickey Mouse" in singlet, shorts and boxing gloves. Number 1588".

Messerschmitt Bf 109E-4/B (W.Nr.1106) of 3./JG53, crash-landed at RAF Manston, Kent, on 17th October 1940. Pilot Oblt. Walter Rupp (Staffelkapitan) was captured unhurt. Two white victory markings ("seigeszeichen") were painted on the port side of the tail-fin.

The RAF crash report for this aircraft stated: "1+ (yellow). Nose and tail orange. Spinner yellow. Large bomb rack fitted".

Messerschmitt Bf 109E-4 (W.Nr.2780) of 6./JG52, crashed at Welling, Kent, on 20th October 1940. Pilot Ofw. Walter Friedmann was killed in action.

Messerschmitt Bf 109E-4 (W.Nr.3548) of 7./JG51, crash-landed at Stonewall Farm, Hunton, Kent, on 25th October 1940. Pilot Fw. Leonhardt Birg was captured unhurt.

The RAF crash report for this aircraft stated: "Markings 4+ green and white spinner. Number 3548. No head armour".

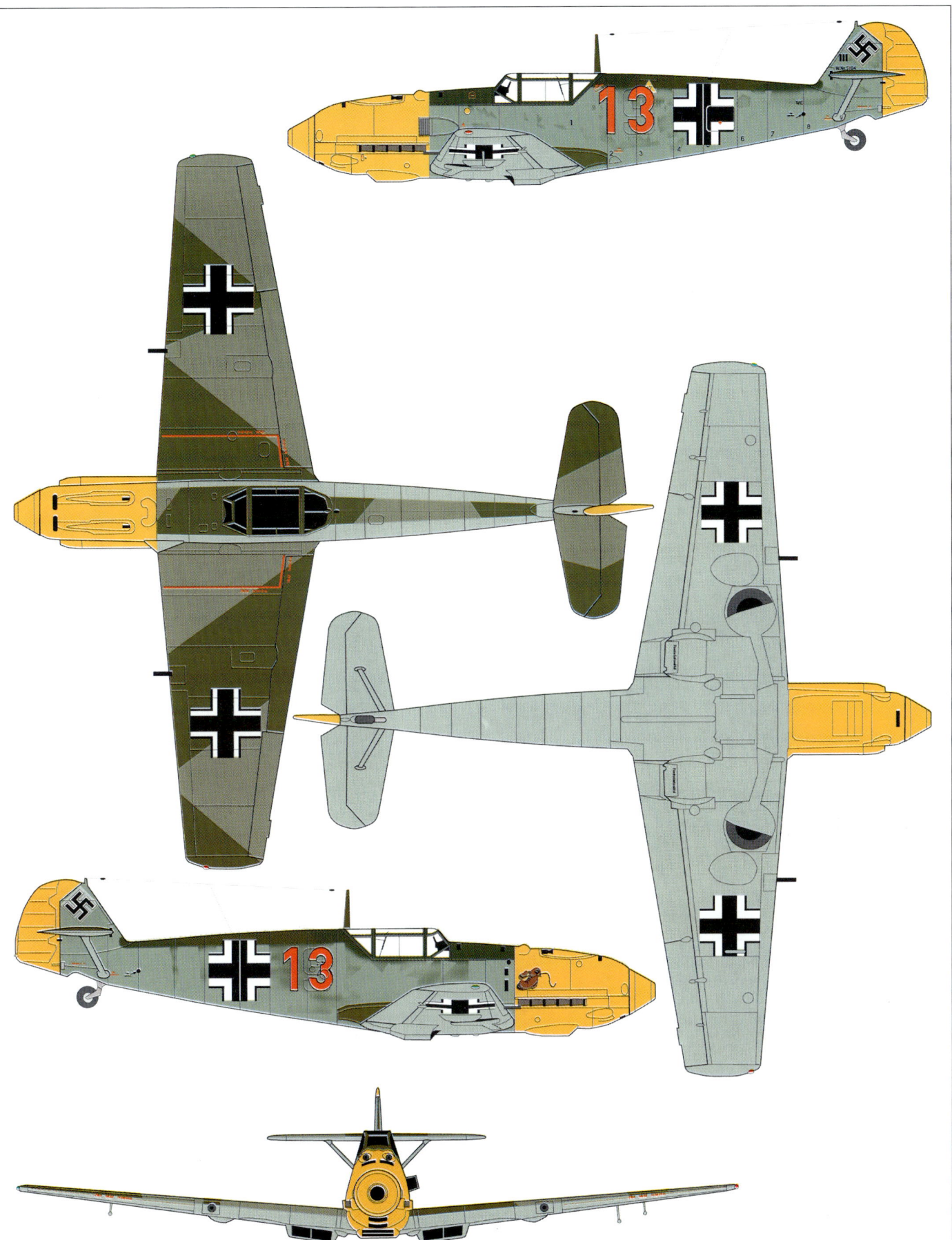

Messerschmitt Bf 109E-4 (W.Nr.5104) of 3./JG77, which crash-landed at Harvey's Cross, Telscombe, Sussex, on 25th October 1940. Pilot Gef. Karl Raisinger was captured uninjured. The fuselage of this aircraft had apparently been originally painted with green uppersurfaces and then had been oversprayed in RLM 65, probably in spring 1940. By the time that this machine came down in Sussex, the light blue paint had eroded in parts to show the underlying greens. The number 13 had been applied over a previous number 9. It would appear that the staffel's "boot" motif was painted on the starboard side of the cowling. The RAF crash report stated "Markings 13+ red. Cowling is yellow and on one side is written in red "Rocho". Works number 5104. Head armour". The aircraft name was not apparent in any of the photographs examined, so is assumed to have been quite small. This machine was subsequently displayed at Rootes Car Showrooms in Maidstone, Kent, where onlookers were allowed to peer into the cockpit, in return for a donation of sixpence to the local "Spitfire Fund".

Messerschmitt Bf 109E-4 (W.Nr.1988) of 5./JG54.
Crash landed at Broomhill, Kent, on 25th. October 1940.
Pilot Oblt. Joachim Schypek was captured unhurt.

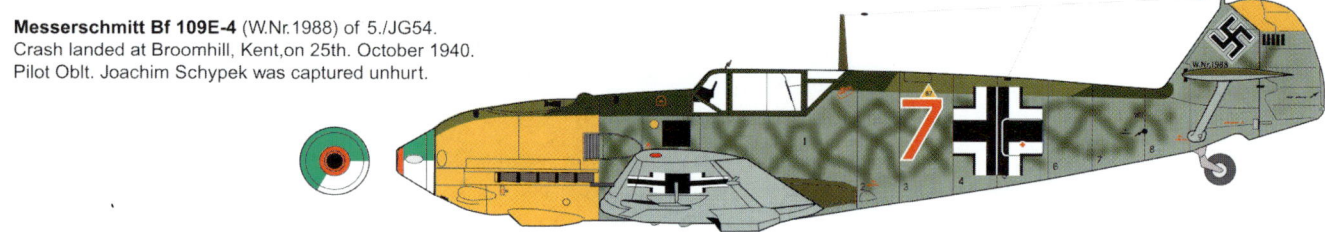

The RAF crash report for this aircraft stated: "Markings:7+ (an old marking of 3+ was just decipherable). Number 1988. Cowling and tip of rudder yellow, spinner green with white flash and red tip".

Messerschmitt Bf 109E-3 (W.Nr.3576) of 7./JG54, crash-landed at Lydd, Kent, on 27th October 1940.
Pilot Uffz. Arno Zimmermann was captured unhurt.

The RAF crash report for this aircraft stated: "Markings 13+ (13 in white, outlined black, the 13 being applied on the fuselage in front of the windscreen and the + halfway down the fuselage. Rudder and nose yellow, spinner white. Crest: a white Dutch clog, edged in black, with wings. Number 3576. The camouflage of the upper surface of the wings is dark grey except for a triangle formed from wing root at trailing edge to a point half way along leading edge. This triangle towards fuselage is a dirty light blue. Fuselage is also dirty light blue dappled with grey".

Messerschmitt Bf 109E-4 (W.Nr.5153) of 9./JG3, crash-landed at Sheperdswell, Kent, on 29th October 1940.
Pilot Oblt. Egon Troha (Staffelkapitan) was captured unhurt.

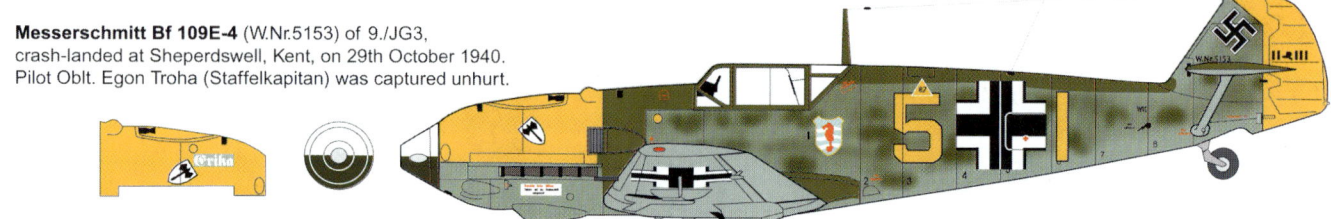

The RAF crash report for this aircraft stated: "Markings 5+I (figures yellow, outlines black). Crest: at side of cockpit, red seahorse on blue ground. On port side of cowling, a double-headed battleaxe in black on white ground. On starboard side, in addition to battleaxe, the word "Erika". Number 5153. Head armour".

Messerschmitt Bf 109E-4/B (W.Nr.5593) of 4./LG2, crash-landed at Langenhoe Wick, Essex, on 29th October 1940.
Pilot Ofw. Josef Harmeling was captured with slight wounds.

The RAF crash report for this aircraft stated: "Markings △ +N (triangle black with white edge, N white with black edge). Crest: black and white Mickey Mouse holding axe in one hand, pistol in other, all on yellow disc. Old markings are still discernable were DH+EJ. Cowling and rudder yellow.
Wingtips had been yellow, but are now covered with green paint.
Spinner white tip and blue and white bands. Bomb rack fitted".

Messerschmitt Bf 109E-1/B of 8./JG3, based at Le Touquet, France, in October 1940.

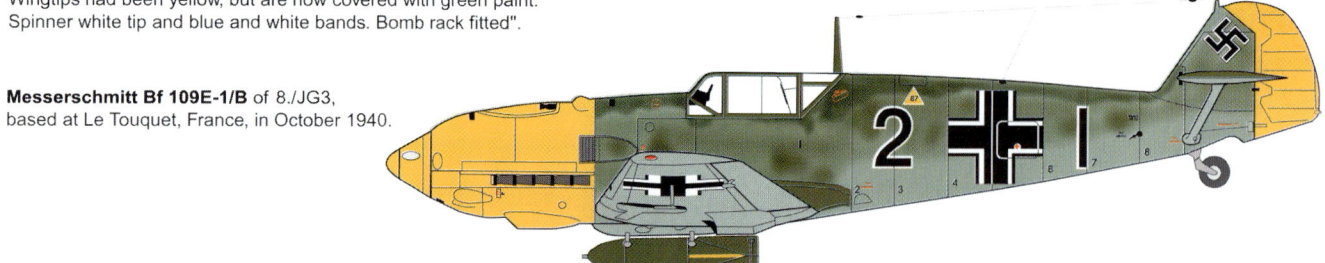

Messerschmitt Bf 109E-4 (W.Nr.1559) of 7./JG27, based at Samer, France, in October 1940.
Pilot Hpt. Wilhelm Balthazar.

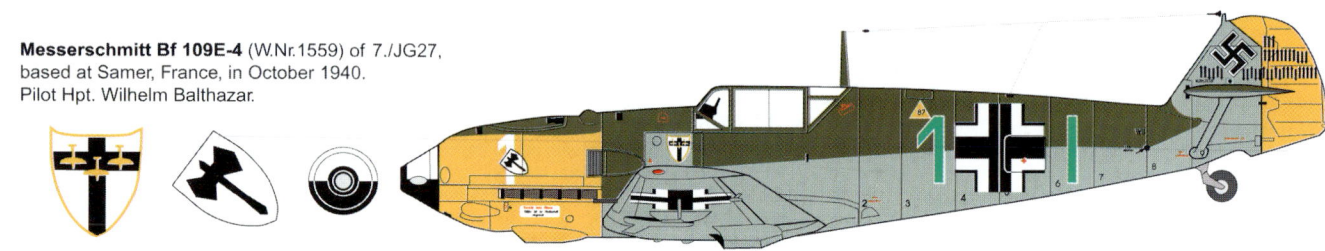

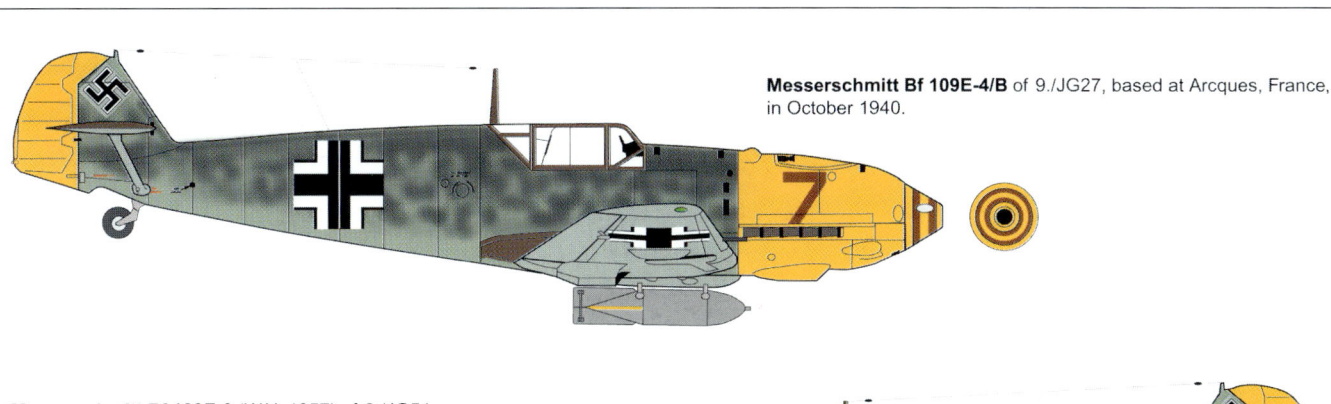

Messerschmitt Bf 109E-4/B of 9./JG27, based at Arcques, France, in October 1940.

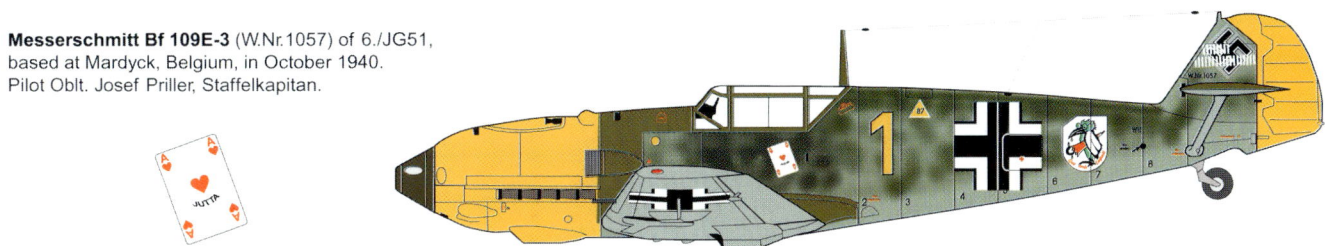

Messerschmitt Bf 109E-3 (W.Nr.1057) of 6./JG51, based at Mardyck, Belgium, in October 1940. Pilot Oblt. Josef Priller, Staffelkapitan.

Messerschmitt Bf 109E-4 of 1./JG52, based at Caffiers, France, in October 1940. Pilot Oblt. Helmut Bennemann.

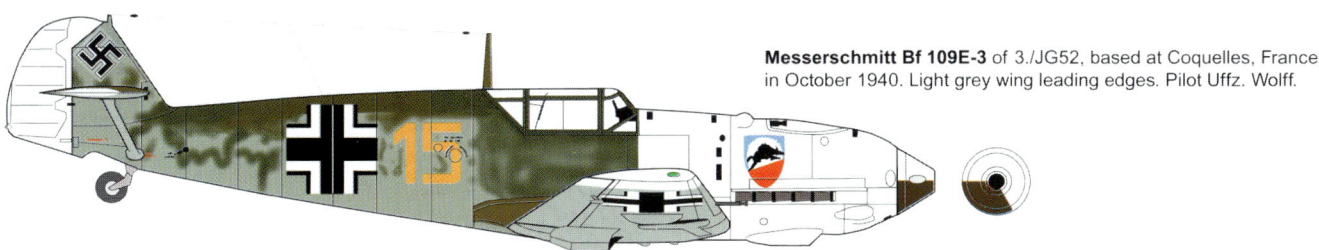

Messerschmitt Bf 109E-3 of 3./JG52, based at Coquelles, France, in October 1940. Light grey wing leading edges. Pilot Uffz. Wolff.

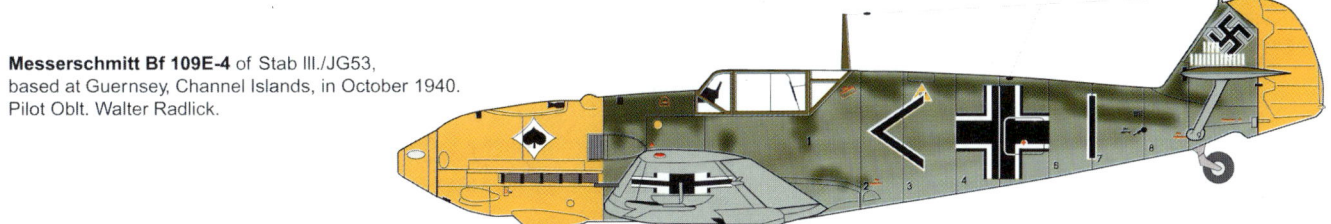

Messerschmitt Bf 109E-4 of Stab III./JG53, based at Guernsey, Channel Islands, in October 1940. Pilot Oblt. Walter Radlick.

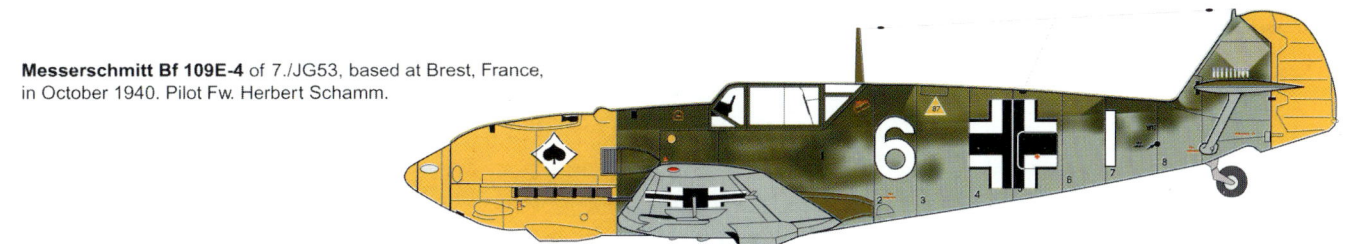

Messerschmitt Bf 109E-4 of 7./JG53, based at Brest, France, in October 1940. Pilot Fw. Herbert Schamm.

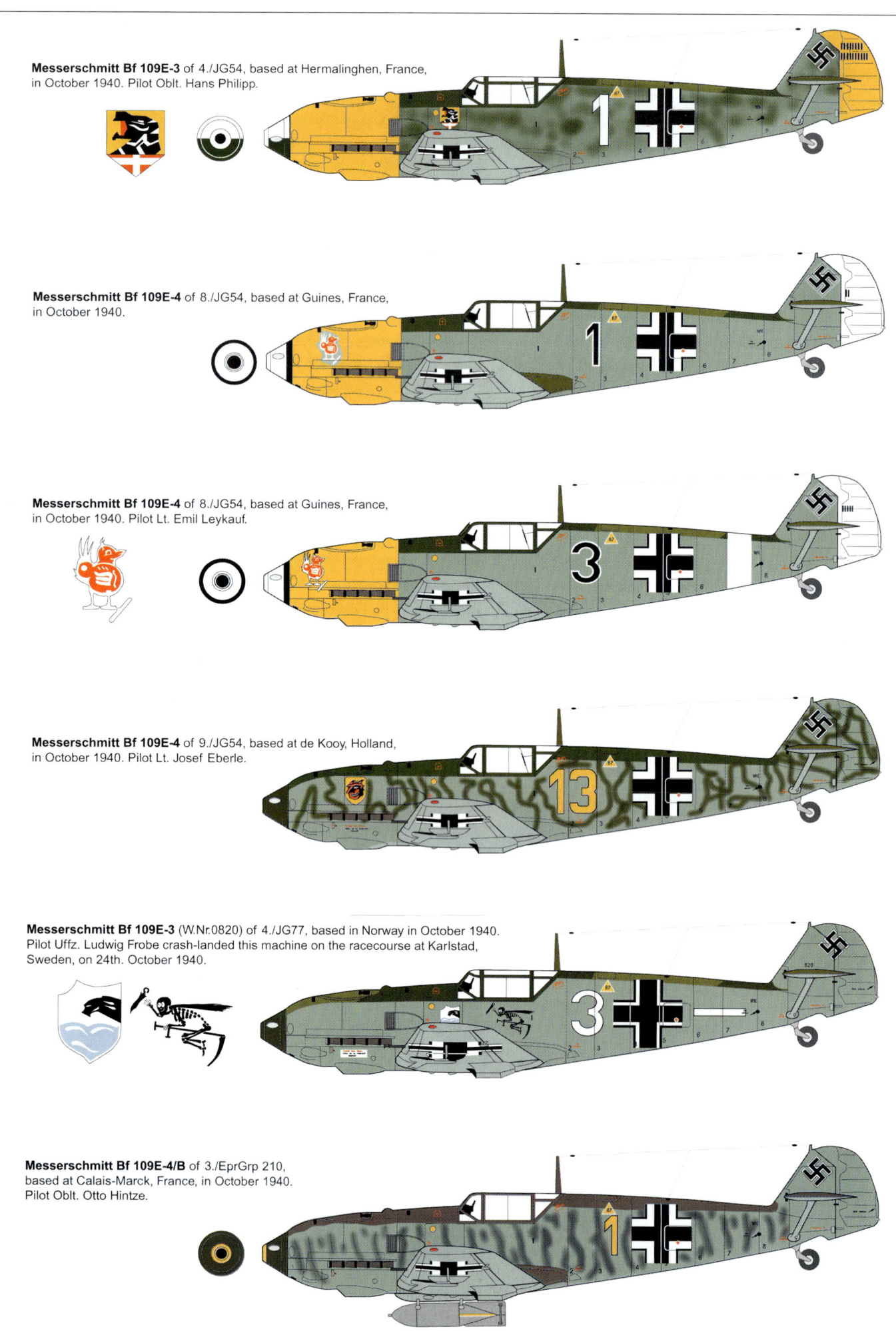

Messerschmitt Bf 109E-3 of 4./JG54, based at Hermalinghen, France, in October 1940. Pilot Oblt. Hans Philipp.

Messerschmitt Bf 109E-4 of 8./JG54, based at Guines, France, in October 1940.

Messerschmitt Bf 109E-4 of 8./JG54, based at Guines, France, in October 1940. Pilot Lt. Emil Leykauf.

Messerschmitt Bf 109E-4 of 9./JG54, based at de Kooy, Holland, in October 1940. Pilot Lt. Josef Eberle.

Messerschmitt Bf 109E-3 (W.Nr.0820) of 4./JG77, based in Norway in October 1940. Pilot Uffz. Ludwig Frobe crash-landed this machine on the racecourse at Karlstad, Sweden, on 24th. October 1940.

Messerschmitt Bf 109E-4/B of 3./EprGrp 210, based at Calais-Marck, France, in October 1940. Pilot Oblt. Otto Hintze.

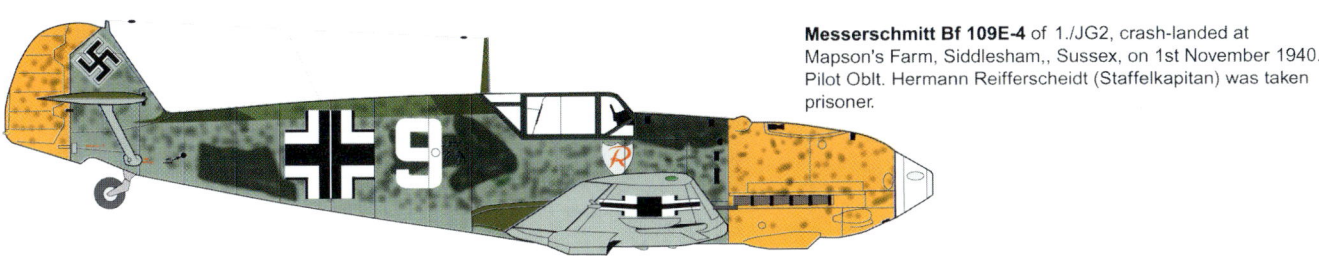

Messerschmitt Bf 109E-4 of 1./JG2, crash-landed at Mapson's Farm, Siddlesham,, Sussex, on 1st November 1940. Pilot Oblt. Hermann Reifferscheidt (Staffelkapitan) was taken prisoner.

The RAF crash report for this aircraft stated: "Markings 9+. Nose and fin of this aircraft dull orange. Red "R" surrounded by red outlined shield on each side of fuselage. The whole of the fuselage is camouflaged very dark mottled olive green".

Messerschmitt Bf 109E-4 of 8./JG2, based at Le Havre, France, in November 1940.

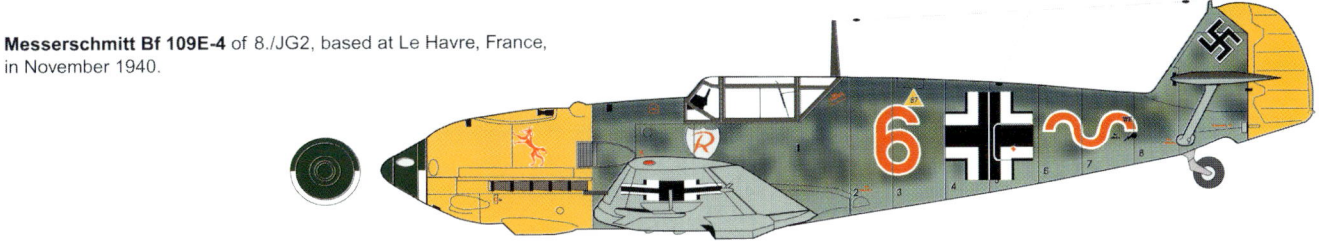

Messerschmitt Bf 109E-4 of 9./JG2, based at Le Havre, France, in November 1940.

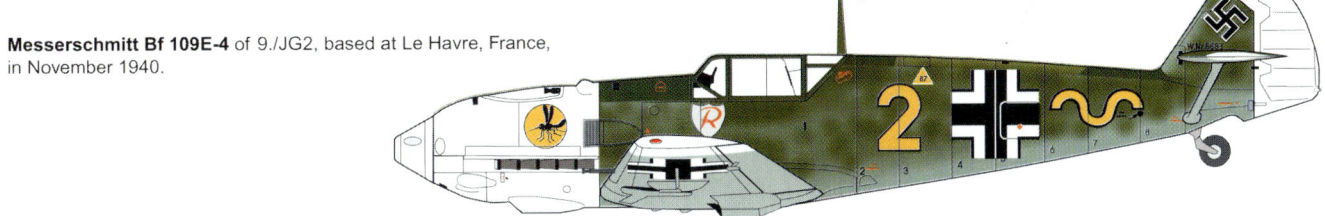

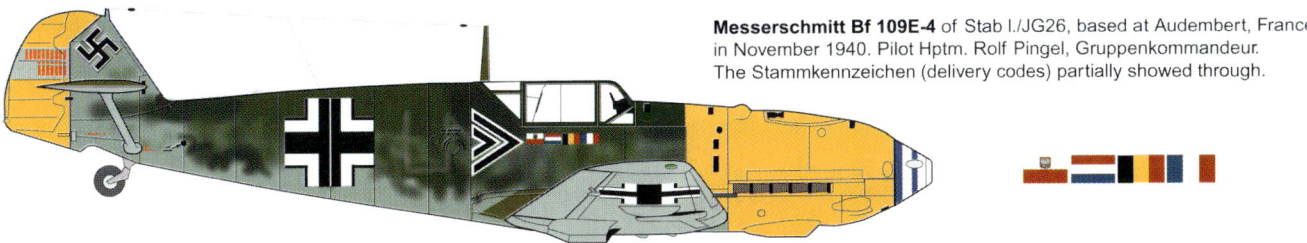

Messerschmitt Bf 109E-4 of Stab I./JG26, based at Audembert, France, in November 1940. Pilot Hptm. Rolf Pingel, Gruppenkommandeur. The Stammkennzeichen (delivery codes) partially showed through.

Messerschmitt Bf 109E-3 of 2./JG26, based at Audembert, France, in November 1940.

Messerschmitt Bf 109E-3 of 2./JG26, based at Audembert, France, in November 1940. Pilot Oblt. Fritz Losigkeit.

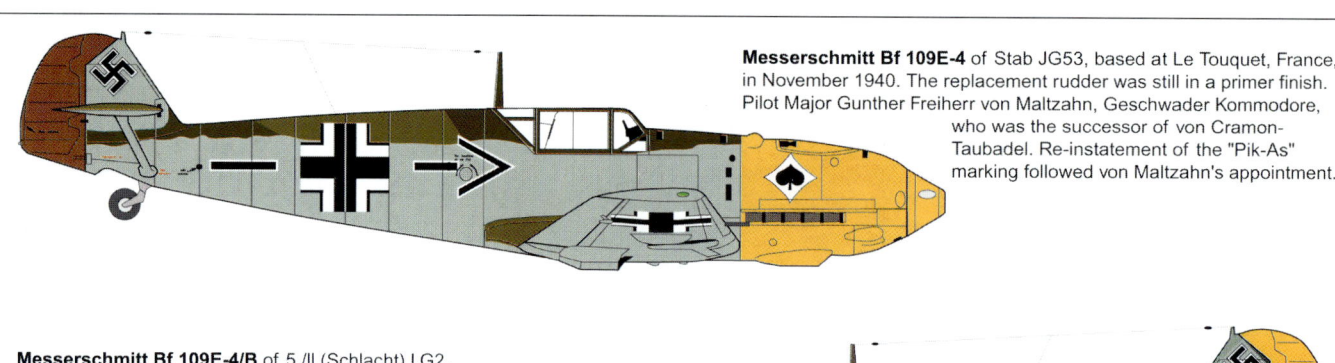

Messerschmitt Bf 109E-4 of Stab JG53, based at Le Touquet, France, in November 1940. The replacement rudder was still in a primer finish. Pilot Major Gunther Freiherr von Maltzahn, Geschwader Kommodore, who was the successor of von Cramon-Taubadel. Re-instatement of the "Pik-As" marking followed von Maltzahn's appointment.

Messerschmitt Bf 109E-4/B of 5./II (Schlacht) LG2, based at Calais-Marck in November 1940. Fitted with an ETC 50 bomb rack and four SC50 bombs.

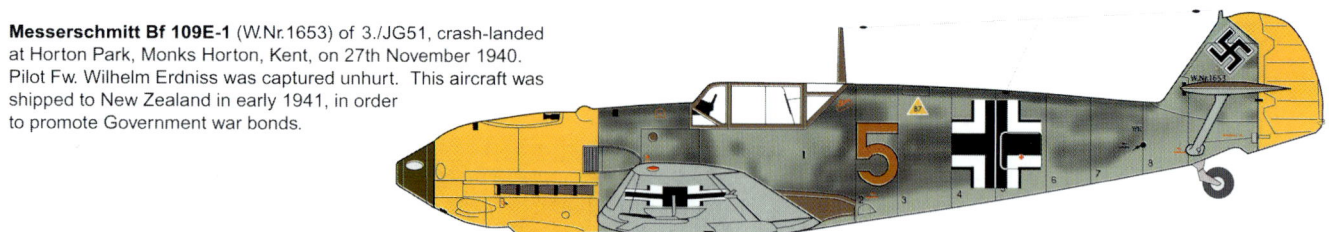

Messerschmitt Bf 109E-1 (W.Nr.1653) of 3./JG51, crash-landed at Horton Park, Monks Horton, Kent, on 27th November 1940. Pilot Fw. Wilhelm Erdniss was captured unhurt. This aircraft was shipped to New Zealand in early 1941, in order to promote Government war bonds.

The RAF crash report for this aircraft stated: "Markings 5+ (5 yellow outlined in black). Head armour". The original cowling from this machine was fitted to Teumer's machine (black 12 on the following page) at RAF St. Athan, in order to make it flyable.

"Brown 5" of 3./JG51, formerly flown by Wilhelm Erdniss, on display in Wellington, New Zealand, in late May 1941. It has been confirmed by three eyewitness reports from New Zealand that this machine was camouflaged in a two-tone grey mottle finish and that the numeral was actually brown 5. Over the years, it has been suggested that this aircraft had white wingtips and aelerons, although these features are not apparent here.

Photo by kind permission of "***The Dominion***". Wellington. New Zealand.

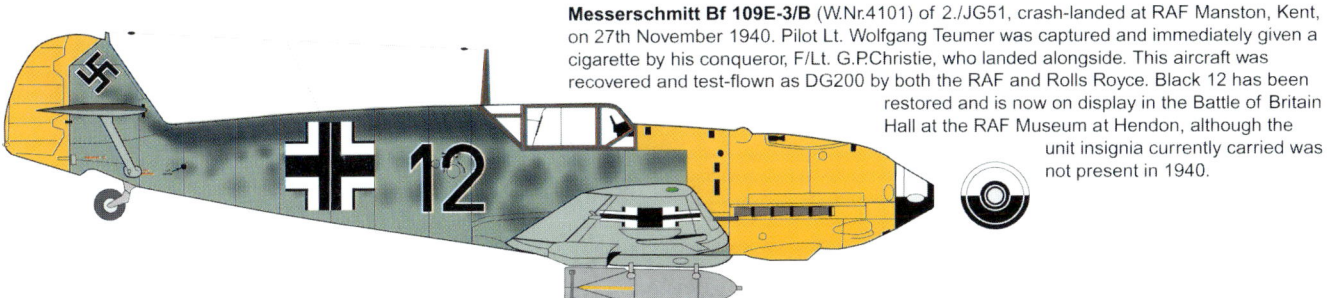

Messerschmitt Bf 109E-3/B (W.Nr.4101) of 2./JG51, crash-landed at RAF Manston, Kent, on 27th November 1940. Pilot Lt. Wolfgang Teumer was captured and immediately given a cigarette by his conqueror, F/Lt. G.P.Christie, who landed alongside. This aircraft was recovered and test-flown as DG200 by both the RAF and Rolls Royce. Black 12 has been restored and is now on display in the Battle of Britain Hall at the RAF Museum at Hendon, although the unit insignia currently carried was not present in 1940.

The RAF crash report for this aircraft stated: "Markings 12+ (the 12 outlined white). Cowling and rudder yellow, spinner green with one white segment. No crest. Number 4101".

Messerschmitt Bf 109E-3 (W.Nr.1289) of 2./JG26, crash-landed at Udimore, Sussex, on 28th November 1940. Pilot Uffz. Heinz Wolf was captured. The retention of the "stammzeichen" on operational aircraft was reportedly quite common, although this is one of the few well documented examples. It is currently on display at the Saxonwold Museum in Johannesburg, South Africa.

The RAF crash report for this aircraft stated: "Markings 2+ (2 in black). An old marking had been painted on this aircraft, the last two letters of which appear to be FA Crest: a devil's face with red mouth and green left eye. Also a black Gothic S on white shield. Nose and rudder yellow. Spinner red. Number 1289. No armour". However, one report contends that only the spinner tip was red, with the remainder being painted in RLM 70.

Messerschmitt Bf 109E-1/B (W.Nr.4900) of 4./JG53, crash-landed at Old Romney, Kent, on 30th November 1940. Pilot Fw. Hermann Schmidt was captured.

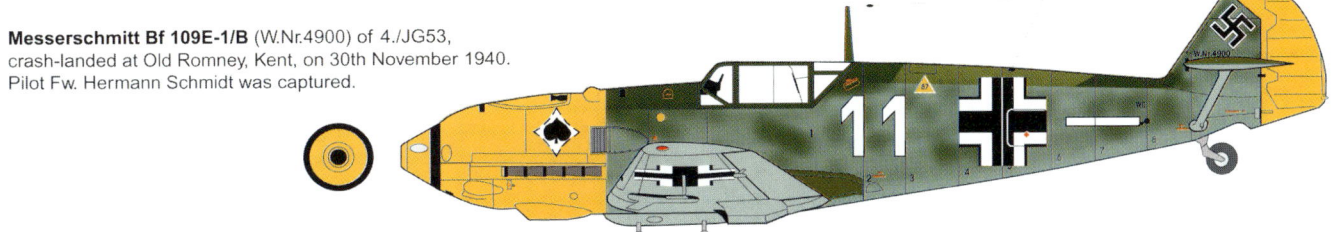

The RAF crash report for this aircraft stated: "Markings 11+- (markings in white). Crest: Ace of Spades in white diamond shield. Number 4900. Large bomb rack".

Messerschmitt Bf 109E-1/B (W.Nr.6313) of 4./LG2. Crash-landed at Woodhyde Farm, Corfe Castle, Dorset, on 30th. November 1940. Pilot Uffz. Paul Wacker was captured.

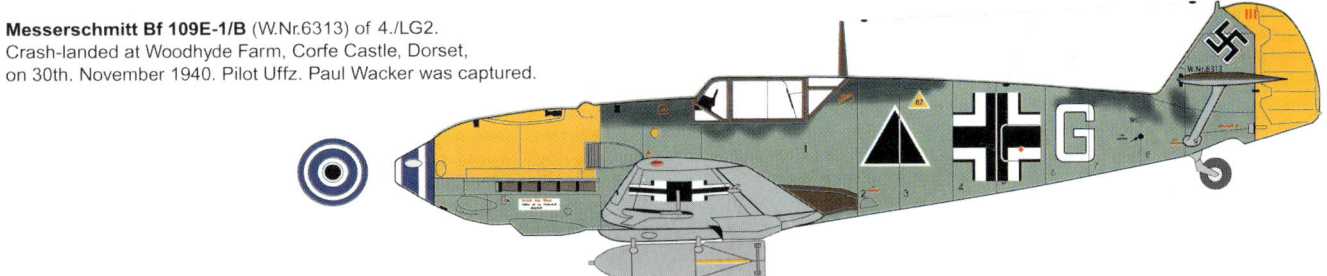

The RAF crash report for this aircraft erroneously stated: "Δ+E (all edged in white). Number 6313".

Messerschmitt Bf 109E-4 of 3./JG1, based in Norway in late 1940.

Messerschmitt Bf 109E-4 of 6./JG77, based at Brest-Guipavas, France, in December 1940. Pilot Oblt. Heinrich Setz.

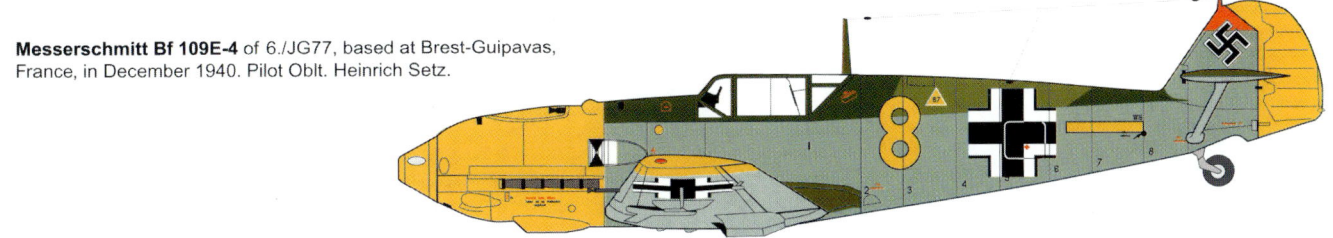

Because of the availability of the RAF crash reports, it was considered to be worthwhile to produce the following twelve profiles of destroyed aircraft, despite lacking photographic evidence of their undamaged condition. This decision was reached on the basis that these were eye-witness statements of markings and the chosen aircraft are unlikely to have been illustrated before. The primary selection criteria for these aircraft was that they were, in some way, different from those that had already been illustrated from photographs. The salient features from each report have been included with typical parent unit markings and the camouflage which other machines were currently wearing. Code size and style were similarly selected.

Messerschmitt Bf 109E-4 (W.Nr.1452) of 4./JG2, shot down at Lympne Castle, Kent, on 2nd September 1940. Pilot Uffz. von Stein was captured. The crash report stated that "Markings 12+- (white outlined black). White rudder and wing tips. Red shield with red letter R on side of fuselage. Completely wrecked".

Messerschmitt Bf 109E-4 (W.Nr.4097) of 9./JG51, shot down at Little Clacton, Essex, on 7th September 1940. Uffz. Koch was captured. The crash report stated "Markings 11+ (yellow). Yellow rudder and cowling and wingtips. Works number 4097. Completely wrecked. No armour".

Messerschmitt Bf 109E-4 (W.Nr.1508) of 1./JG53, shot down in flames near the Old Jail Inn, Biggin Hill, Kent, on 9th September 1940. Fw. Honisch was captured. Although this aircraft was supposed to be white 5, the crash report stated that "Markings + only. Red band round engine cowling. Totally destroyed. Two cannon in wreckage, but no M.G. Camouflage standard. No white on wing tips. Spinner dark green".

Messerschmitt Bf 109E-4 (W.Nr.5116) of 9./JG54, shot down at Golden Green, Kent, on 30th September 1940. Uffz. Braatz was killed. In contrast to the yellow number to be expected, the crash report stated that "Markings were a large 6 in black, outlined yellow. Complete wreck".

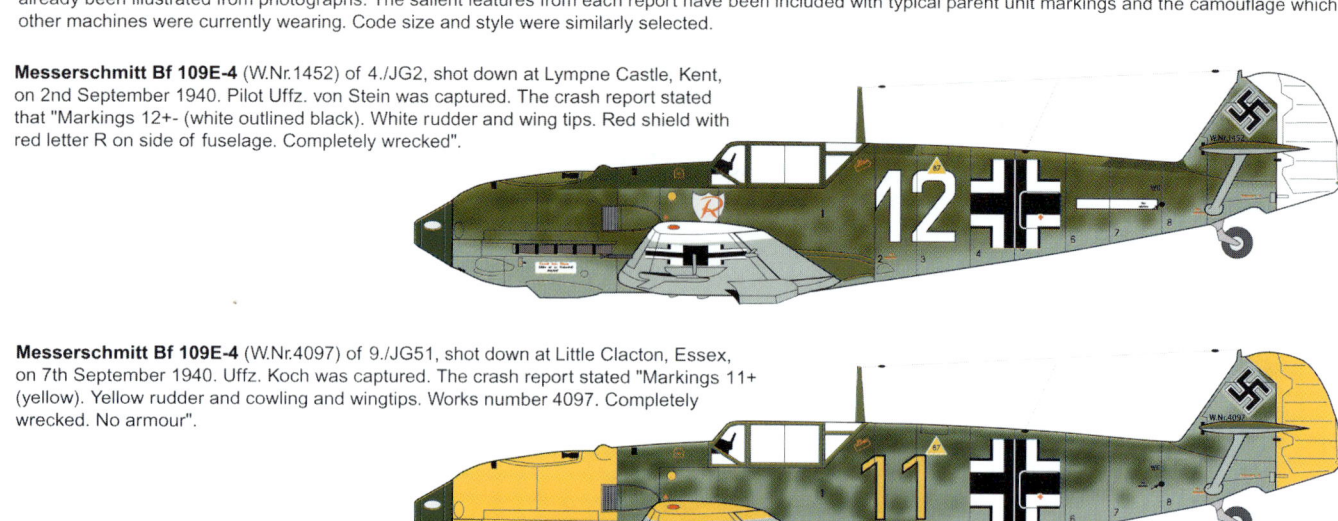

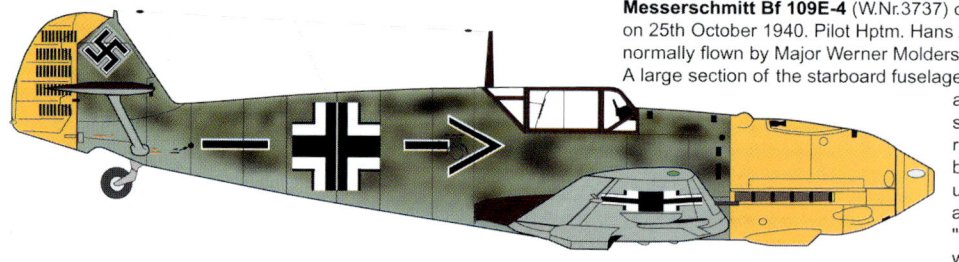

Messerschmitt Bf 109E-4 (W.Nr.3737) of Stab JG51, exploded over Marden, Kent, on 25th October 1940. Pilot Hptm. Hans Asmus baled out wounded. This aircraft was normally flown by Major Werner Molders and carried his Kommodore markings. A large section of the starboard fuselage is on display at the Lashenden Air Museum and is RLM 02 overall, with large and crudely sprayed patches of RLM 61. The RAF crash report stated "Following fighter action, pilot baled out at a great height and aircraft broke up in the air. Wreckage was distributed over a very wide area. There were 49 so-called "victory" stripes on the tail. Airscrew blades were covered with ice when the aircraft crashed".

Messerschmitt Bf 109E-7 (W.Nr.4124) of Stab I./JG3, shot down at West Wickham, Kent, on 27th October 1940. Lt. Busch (Gruppe Nachr. Offz) baled out and was captured wounded. The crash report stated that "<-+ black with white outline. Works number 4124. No pilot head armour. Complete wreck".

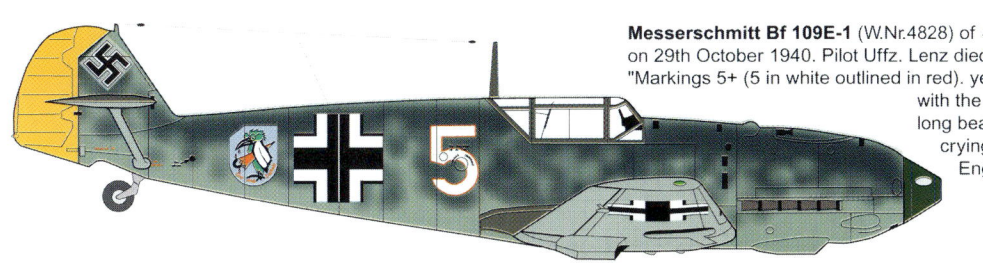

Messerschmitt Bf 109E-1 (W.Nr.4828) of 4./JG54, shot down at Horsham, Sussex, on 29th October 1940. Pilot Uffz. Lenz died of his injuries. The crash report stated "Markings 5+ (5 in white outlined in red). yellow rudder. Crest on a light blue shield with the corner broken off, a parrot-like bird with a long beak with a red umbrella under left wing. Bird crying. Under the shield, the words "Gott strafe England" in red. Completely wrecked".

Messerschmitt Bf 109E-4 (W.Nr.5370) of 4./JG54, shot down at Langton Green, Kent, on 29th October 1940. Pilot Lt. Tornow was killed. The crash report stated "Markings 9+ (9 in white outlined in red). Crest on this aircraft is same as above. Nose yellow. Spinner dark green. Completely wrecked". This aircraft and white 5 above were shot down within minutes of each other and indicate how the yellow tactical markings differed within a unit. The eye-witness report of the light blue unit markings provides yet another variation.

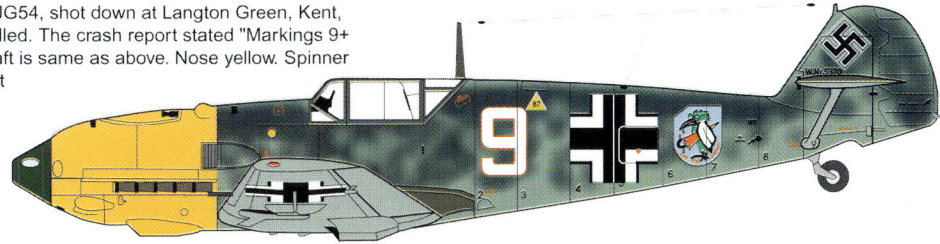

Messerschmitt Bf 109E-1 (W.Nr.6360) of 6./JG3, shot down at Meopham, Kent, on 30th October 1940. Pilot Uffz. Fahrian baled out slightly wounded. The RAF crash report stated "Markings +- (minus sign yellow, outlined black)". No mention was made of the numeral 9, so the assumption here is that the fuselage had disintegrated forwards of the fuselage cross. The report was more interested in aircraft armament and recorded four MG17s found in the wreckage, indicating that this aircraft was an E-1 variant, rather than the E-4 as indicated by the Werk Number.

Messerschmitt Bf 109E-4/B (W.Nr.3740) of 9./JG26, crashed at Wittersham, Kent, on 5th November 1940. Pilot Lt. Heinz Ebeling (Staffelkapitan) baled out and was taken prisoner. The RAF crash report stated " Markings I+ There is a further letter or figure not decipherable. The I is in yellow outlined in black. Crest: a black winged demon encircled in red. Complete wreck. No pilot armour. Fitted for carriage of a 250Kg bomb". Parts of this aircraft are held in the Battle of Britain Museum at Hawkinge, including the rudder, which is painted in RLM 27 gelb, with the victory marks in RLM 23 rot.

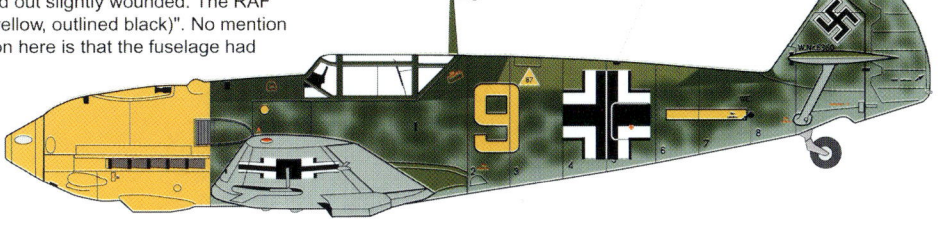

Messerschmitt Bf 109E-1/B (W.Nr.3259) of 9./JG26, crashed at Wittersham, Kent, on 5th November 1940. Pilot Uffz. Walter Braun baled out at about 13,000 feet and was taken prisoner. The crash report clearly stated: " Markings I+11 both figures in yellow with no black outline. Engine cowling and fin yellow. In collision with machine above. Four MG17. Fitted for carriage of 250Kg bomb". Yet a photograph of the wreckage of this machine clearly shows that both 11 and the 3 gruppe bar were outlined in black.

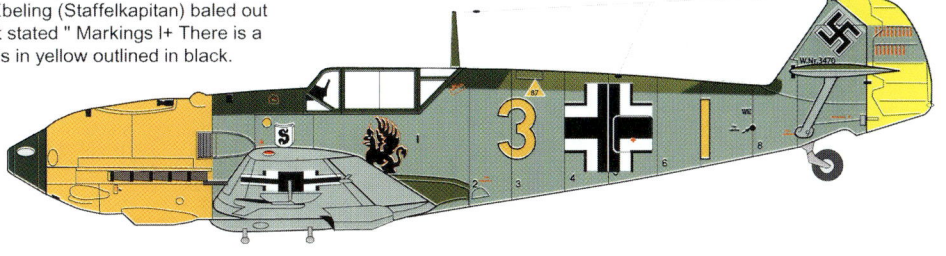

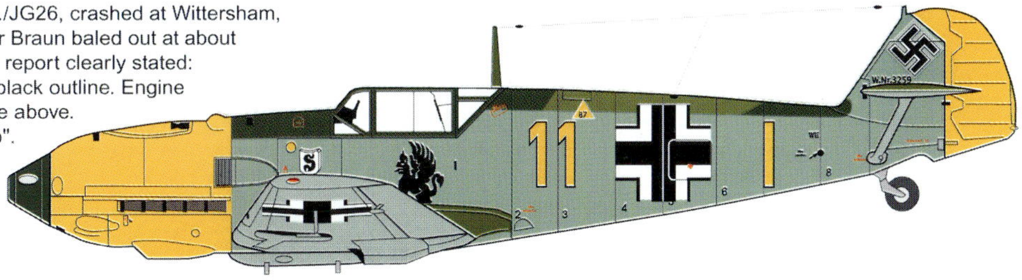

Messerschmitt Bf 109E-1 (W.Nr.4010) of 5./JG53, attempted a crash-landing at Smeeth Railway Station, Kent, on 23rd November 1940, but flew through some trees and removed both wings. Pilot Lt. Otto Zauner captured. The RAF crash report stated: " Markings 12+ (12 in blue with white edge). Crest on side of cowling is Ace of Spades on a white diamond outlined black. Spinner red. Four MG17. Struck trees whilst landing and wrecked".

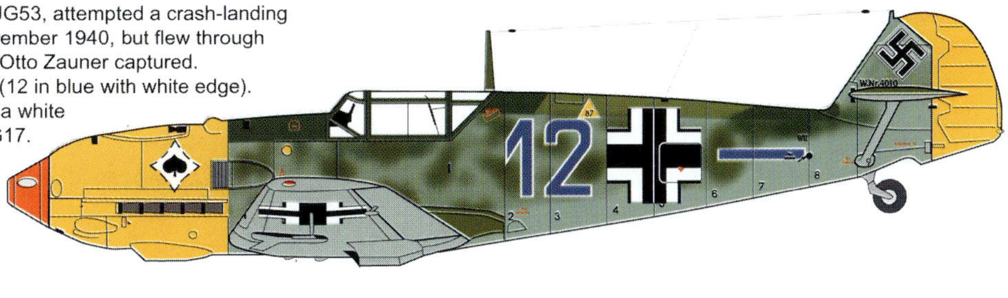

Above: Bf 109E-3, 'white 7' of 1./JG 2 'Richthofen', being re-armed in the open. The 'Bonzo Dog' *Staffel* badge can just be seen behind the intake fairing on the cowling panel that has been moved forward and is resting on the exhausts. Note the rag-applied 'stipple' mottle common to this unit's aircraft.

identical even within the same units, and even varied in colour between aircraft. As with the unit badges, some of the personal artwork had 'history', having been carried on aircraft active in Spain with the *Condor Legion*. In the case of JG 53 'Pik As', the unit badge, the Ace of Spades, was painted out and replaced by a red band around the cowling on the orders of Goering, for reasons which are explained later.

Like all *Luftwaffe* aircraft, Bf 109s were originally delivered from the factory bearing large letters on either side of the fuselage crosses. Known as *'stamkennzeichen'*, these factory registration letters were generally overpainted or removed prior to the application of *Staffel* numerals/letters or *Stab* markings. Nevertheless, some continued to show through on some machines and aircraft are reported

Above left: Bf 109E-4, 'white 7' of 7./JG 2 'Richthofen', dispersed in the open at Beaumont-le-Roger. The rudder is perhaps white, although yellow was far more usual. The spinner tip was white.

Left: Possibly a Bf 109E-7, also of 7./JG 2, but fitted with a fuselage centre-line mounted 250kg bomb. The array of rudder 'kill' tabs point to it being 'white 15' (*w.nr* 5983), in which Werner Machold was shot down over Swanage on 9 June 1941. (M W Payne Collection)

52

On 5 September 1940, **Messerschmitt Bf109E-4, W.Nr.1096,** which was white 6 of 1./JG 54, provided part of the fighter escort for a bomber force operating over the Thames Estuary. Its pilot, *Uffz* Fritz Hotzelmann, was flying as wingman to the *Gruppe Kommandeur, Hauptman* von Bonin.

The *Luftwaffe* crews were engaged by the Spitfires of 19 Squadron near Chatham and this aircraft was damaged by F/O L A Haines. Its pilot flew inland at very low level over north Kent, pursued by the Spitfire, which repeatedly scored hits, both to the cooling system and to the engine, which ultimately caught fire. *Uffz* Hotzelmann then climbed to about 800 feet and baled out, falling alongside his aircraft until his parachute partially deployed at about 400 feet, to the cheers of onlookers on the ground.

His aircraft crashed onto this house in Hardy Street, Maidstone in Kent whose four occupants were fortunately sitting-out the raid in the cellar. The pilot landed on the roof of a house about 250 yards away and broke both of his legs as he toppled into the street below, since his partially deployed parachute had collapsed on his initial landing.

Although this is an intriguing cameo, why is a scene of destruction, almost aviation-free apart from some wreckage, of interest in a discussion on aircraft markings ?

The answer lies in the RAF Crash Report, which stated:- "Top of rudder and tailplanes apparently painted white. Burnt out". This statement, together with the photograph of the wreckage, provides another and apparently unique set of tactical markings.

As an aside, this scene is within 60 yards of the perimeter wall of Maidstone Prison. The gable extension has long since been rebuilt, but it is completely different to those of the other houses in the street.

Photo courtesy of Kent Messenger.

to have flown operationally with these factory registration letters still visible, particularly on the machine flown by *Uffz* Wolf of 2./JG 26 - now on display in South Africa.

Camouflage

At the end of 1939, the predominant *Luftwaffe* fighter colour scheme was *Schwarzgrun* 70/*Dunkelgrun* 71 uppersurfaces in a hard-edged splinter pattern with *Hellblau* 65 undersurfaces, where the upper surfaces were well camouflaged against a woodland background. However, as the *Luftwaffe* confronted French and British aircraft over a winter landscape, it was found that the dark upper surfaces actually compromised the aircraft.

During the invasion of France and the Low Countries in the spring of 1940, it was noticed by allied aircrew that many Bf 109Es had adopted a revised colour scheme, which included the repainting of the black-green *Schwarzgrun* 70 areas with the grey-green *Grau* 02 colour. The pale grey-blue *Hellblau* 65 undersurface colour was also extended up the fuselage

Right: Bf 109E-1/B, 'black 12' of 2.(J)/LG 2, force-landed in the Calais-Marck region. The numeral '1' appears to be a later addition to make the number '12'. Note the 'top hat' *Staffel* badge on a white disc on the rear fuselage.
(C Goss via M W Payne)

sides on to a line level with the canopy sill, or even higher to leave just the fuselage spine in the original colours, and entirely covering the fin and rudder. Spinners generally remained in *Schwarzgrun* 70, or were partially or entirely, repainted in the *Staffel* or *Gruppe* colour(s).

Both the original and the new styles continued in use until the fall of France in June 1940. However, by that stage, some units had found that the large areas of light grey-blue *Hellblau* 65 was *too* conspicuous and that they required a

greater degree of camouflage and applied soft mottling or rag-applied stippling over the fuselage sides. Some of the earlier applications of pale grey-blue up the fuselage sides had also eroded sufficiently for the original two-tone dark greens to show through, which had a similar effect.

Appreciating that further problems with camouflage would arise as their fighters flew across the English Channel, unit applied mottle applications became the norm. Different units adopted different styles and it is understood that

Above: Helmut Wick's 'yellow 2' (W.Nr 5344), of 3./JG 2 as it looked at the end of August 1940. He used this machine until his death on 28 November 1940, marked in turn with *Gruppenkommandeur* then *Geschwader Kommodore Stab* markings.

Left: 'Yellow 8' (W.Nr 1588), flown by *Obfw* Franz Jaenisch, also of 3./JG 2, photographed in June 1940.

Below: 'White 5' of 7./JG 53, flown by Hans-Georg Schulte, shot down on 6 September 1940.
Note the fuselage mottle, and modified fuselage crosses on all three of these aircraft. (M W Payne Collection)

these styles were generally decided upon at *Kommodore* level.

By the time of the opening stages of the Battle of Britain proper in late July/early August 1940, *Schwarzgrun* 70/*Dunkelgrun* 71 uppersurfaces were the exception, and the *Dunkelgrun* 71/*Grau* 02 uppersurface scheme was firmly established, albeit with minor variations including various uppersurface camouflage patterns which weren't so 'splintered' or 'hard-edged'.

As combats over the English Channel reached heights in excess of 20,000ft, a more suitable 'high altitude' scheme was required, and it is believed that the application of the three 'mid-war' fighter greys appear to have been introduced much earlier than had previously been thought, in preference to the greens. The *Farbton Dunkelgrau* 74/ *Mittelgrau* 75/ *Hellgrau* 76 combination has frequently been asserted not to have been introduced before the November 1941 edition of the *Luftwaffe's* L Dv 521/1 paint chart was released, but personal examination of wreckage from the Battle of Britain has revealed that a

Right: 'Yellow 8' of 9./JG 2, almost certainly being flown by Rudi Rothenfelder, date uncertain, but before the yellow cowlings appeared at the end of August. (M W Payne Collection)

Left: Bf 109E-1, 'yellow 5' of 9./JG 2, based at Charleville, France in June 1940. Note how the fuselage cross has been covered over with netting to provide a degree of camouflage whilst dispersed in the open. (M W Payne Collection)

combination of grey paint in shades very similar to the 74/75/76 Farbton colours had been applied to many of the aircraft involved.

A plausible explanation for the lack of any *Luftwaffe* paint charts between 1939 and November 1941, which may have identified the actual introduction dates of the 74/75/76 greys has been offered, in that on the acceptance of ultimate defeat in 1945, Goering ordered that all *Luftwaffe* documentation should be destroyed. Since more than enough manpower was available, document destruction was more complete (90-95%) within the *Luftwaffe* than the other services.

Of course none of these changes were affected overnight, there being evidence to suggest that 71/02/65 finished Bf 109Es were operational shortly before the fighting in Poland had ceased, and certainly the scheme appears to have been in widespread use before the 1940 'Blitzkrieg' offensive, as contemporary photographs taken in the rather cold, early spring, show. A mixed assortment of colours from the original green shades and the 'new' grey shades was not uncommon; wing and tailplane uppersurfaces in 71/02 and the fuselage spine in 74/75, or just one of the grey colours being a frequently recorded variation. Even when the uppersurfaces were entirely overpainted in 74/75 over the 71/02, the 'original' *Hellblau* 65 undersurfaces were often retained, and although the 71/02/65 scheme was still the predominant scheme throughout the Battle of Britain period, as the summer passed in to autumn, and autumn in to winter, the percentage of 74/75/76 (or 65) finished *Emils* increased.

National insignia had also gone through a change in late 1939/early 1940. The fuselage and underwing crosses (*Balkenkreuze*) received wider white borders, and the swastika (*Hakenkreuz*) was repositioned fully on to the fin from its previous location centrally across the fin and rudder hinge line.

Tactical markings

As an aid to rapid identification of friend

Right: Bf 109E-3, 'black 3' of 8./JG 53, photographed in July or August 1940. Note the red spinner and red band around the cowling. JG 53 were renowned for their imaginative use of camouflage colours, the fuselage of this particular example being no exception. (M W Payne)

from foe, was the liberal use of yellow, and to a somewhat lesser degree, white, paint or temporary distemper - removeable by washing off with aviation fuel. Some of the air leaders had started to personalize their aircraft for identification purposes as early as late July, eg *Oblt* Bartels, and *Oberstlt* Vick with a yellow rudder and white cowling respectively.

As the tempo of the Battle of Britain increased, so did the need to find a solution to rapid identification of friendly aircraft. The initial *Luftwaffe* solution in the middle of August was to paint the tip of the rudder yellow, although a few units painted the entire rudder. By the end of August, cowlings, rudders, wing tips and tailplane tips were commonly painted yellow or, less frequently, white, but by no means were *all* of these recognition features applied to *every* aircraft.

Naturally, plenty of anomalies arose. At the end of September, *Gefr* Mummert of 4./JG 52 force-landed his aircraft at RAF Detling, where it was found to be *still* painted in its original 1939 colour scheme of 70/71/65, and towards the end of the year, certain members of the *Jagdflieger* evidently believed that the yellow paintwork was now *too* conspicuous and elected to overpaint or remove it, eg *Oblt* Reifferscheidt's '*Emil*' of 1./JG 2.

The profiles

The colours of the earlier aircraft were relatively easy to determine, since they were not that far removed from their 1939 schemes, which are relatively well documented. As far as the mottled fuselage side camouflage is concerned, it is almost impossible to tell *which* colours were used. An examination of the samples of greens and greys, when reduced to monochrome, are practically identical. The blue/greys, Farbton 65 and 76, are so close in monochrome reproduction anyway as to virtually defy identification from a sixty year-old b&w photograph or, worse, a poorly reproduced copy of a sixty year-old b&w photograph.

The colours of the profiles were therefore deduced by examination of photographs and personal records made in England by individuals at the time. These deductions were made in conjunction with physical observations of wreckage at various museums and in the personal collections of individuals in Kent and Sussex and by comparison with the relevant RAF crash report.

These crash reports were obtained from the Public Record Office at Kew, specifically from File AIR 22/266, titled 'AMWR Location of Enemy Aircraft Brought Down in the UK - Reports 1-124 August to December 1940'. This file was evidently an amalgam of many reports submitted by individual RAF Officers, who were specifically tasked to examine wreckage, with a view to obtaining technical information about additional armour plate, engines, weapons etc. However, from the point of view of intelligence, they frequently recorded details of colour schemes and unit badges, or any other detail that they felt extraordinary and that they had found during the course of their examinations.

These reports have been quoted whenever possible, immediately adjacent to each relevant profile. The files were intended to be submitted on a daily basis

Left: Autumn mists at Le Touquet, as 7./JG 53 taxi out for another sortie. Note the re-instated 'Pik As' (Ace of Spades) *Staffel* badge, and the reduced style of fuselage *balkenkreuz* (cross).

Below: November at Le Touquet with 7./JG 53. These aircraft most probably had the swastikas painted over. The pointed-capped spinners suggest that they might be Bf 109E-7s. (M W Payne Collection)

and almost inevitably contain obvious errors which, where possible, have been identified.

The crash reports also reveal some interesting areas of detail, such as recording the use of 'orange' (sic) nose colours and yellow codes. The assumption here is that the yellow tactical nose colouration was consistently *Gelb* 04 and the yellow numeral was, in certain cases, *Gelb* 27. They also recorded the aircrafts' *Werke Nummern*, (works or construction numbers), any differences in unit markings and the colour of the codes wherever possible.

In many cases, especially involving those aircraft that had force-landed, what proved to be an insurmountable hurdle was in determining whether they had head armour or not. The reason here was that, in the vast majority of cases, the canopy had understandably been jettisoned by the pilot prior to the force-landing, in order to ease his escape from his aeroplane's cockpit.

No real attempt has been made to portray any exhaust stains on the profiles, particularly on those aircraft that were recovered practically intact. In many cases, they had sustained damage to the engine cooling systems, which had overheated and then emitted boiling oil from every engine aperture prior to crash-landing. These stains are evident in many of the photographs of captured machines.

As far as possible, the colour profiles have been arranged in date order, as a means of displaying the progressive applications of camouflage, tactical markings and increased victory tallies. This progression is particularly evident on a couple of individual machines, which have been deliberately illustrated twice.

Above: *Oblt* Walter Stengel's 'yellow 10' of 6./JG 51. The badge with three birds was to record his glider pilot's C-Award. He later became the unit's *Staffelkapitan*.

Right: The tail of Josef Priller's 'yellow 1' (*w.nr* 5057), in its *splitterbox* at Pihen, when he was *Staffelkapitan* of 6./JG 51. Note the twenty-one 'kill' tabs painted over the swastika. (M W Payne Collection)